THE PODCAST BOOK
2018

ORLANDO RIOS

PODCASTING PRO

The Podcast Book
2018

Copyright © 2018 by Orlando Rios Publishing

ISBN-13: 978-0692045053
ISBN-10: 0692045058

Podcasting Pro
www.podcastingpro.com
info@podcastingpro.com

Follow:

@orlandorios
@podcastingpro

/orlandoriospage
/podcastingpro

Printed in U.S.A

CONTENTS

WELCOME TO THE PODCAST BOOK

Since the last edition of *The Podcast Book*, the amount of people that have listened to a podcast in the US has grown another 40%, which equates to about 112 million new addicts of this entertainment we all know and love.

With the growth of listeners also comes growth in content producers. Thanks to inexpensive home personal recording equipment (and hopefully my *Podcasting Pro Basics* book), almost anyone has the power to express themselves and let their voice be heard on this platform. In fact, I bet you have a friend that has had an idea for, or has published their own podcast. Or maybe that friend is you?

This is why I love podcasts so much.

In a world where it seems only those with the biggest pockets or the best connections can get their stories to the public, podcasts provide an open door. It costs nothing to publish or listen to a podcast. There are no government regulations on podcasts. The only limit is your imagination... and time.

Hence the creation of *The Podcast Book*.

Great for the podcast newbie or lover, this book is a directory of what iTunes (and myself) interpret to be the best podcasts in the world. If you've ever scrolled *Netflix* aimlessly in search of a program, you will eventually come to the same problem with podcasts. Because of this, I've tried to make your search easier by listing these shows in a simple and easy-to-digest format.

In every category you will find the top pick for the year, along with thirty other chart toppers that have displayed unique popularity. To help you get a quick glance of each podcast, I've included information on the host, frequency, runtime, and the listed description for the program. Plus new in this year's edition, I've added the *You May Also Like* feature which will help you discover shows similar to the ones you already love!

So go have fun finding a new favorite podcast. I suggest taking a highlighter and marking the listings that interest you most. Then most importantly, sit back, listen, and enjoy your findings.

Happy Listening,
Orlando Rios

ARTS

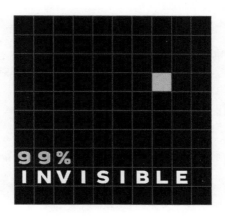

2018 Arts Top Pick
99% Invisible
Host: Roman Mars
Frequency: Daily
Average Show Length: 30 Minutes

Design is everywhere in our lives, perhaps most importantly in the places where we've just stopped noticing. 99% Invisible is a weekly exploration of the process and power of design and architecture. From award winning producer Roman Mars.

You May Also Like:
Invisibilia, Radiolab, Reply All, Planet Money,
More Perfect

Fresh Air
Host: Terry Gross
Frequency: Daily
Average Show Length: 50 Minutes

Description:
Fresh Air from WHYY, the Peabody Award-winning weekday magazine
of contemporary arts and issues, is one of public radio's most
popular programs. Hosted by Terry Gross, the show features intimate
conversations with today's biggest luminaries.

You May Also Like:
This American Life, Radio Lab, The Moth, Revisionist History, The Daily

The Moth
Host: Various
Frequency: Weekly
Average Show Length: 50 Minutes

Description:
Since its launch in 1997, The Moth has presented thousands of true stories,
told live and without notes, to standing-room-only crowds worldwide. Moth
storytellers stand alone, under a spotlight, with only a microphone and a
roomful of strangers. The storyteller and the audience embark on a high-
wire act of shared experience which is both terrifying and exhilarating.

You May Also Like:
Radiolab, Invisibilia, This American Life, Fresh Air, Wait Wait... Don't Tell Me!

Deadly Manners
Host: LeVar Burton
Frequency: Weekly
Average Show Length: 30 Minutes
Chaptered Series (2017)

Description:
Deadly Manners is a 10 episode, dark comedy murder-mystery series set
in the winter of 1954. It follows the events during the night of the affluent
Billings family annual dinner party with their distinguished, eccentric
guests. However, all is not fun and games as shortly after the party starts,
a snowstorm begins to rage outside, trapping all the partygoers inside
their host's mansion. When a murderer starts killing off those in

attendance, the guests must figure out who is responsible, or at least how to stay alive -- lest they be next.

You May Also Like:
A Murder On Orchard Street, Rabbits, Cults, Archive 8, Dark Tome

Homecoming
Host: N/A
Frequency: Weekly
Average Show Length: 30 Minutes
Seasoned Series (2016, 2017)

Description:
The first scripted series from Gimlet Media, starring Catherine Keener, Oscar Isaac, David Schwimmer, David Cross, Amy Sedaris, Michael Cera, Mercedes Ruehl, Alia Shawkat, Chris Gethard, and Spike Jonze. Homecoming centers on a caseworker at an experimental facility, her ambitious supervisor, and a soldier eager to rejoin civilian life — presented in an enigmatic collage of telephone calls, therapy sessions, and overheard conversations.

You May Also Like:
Limetown, LifeAfter, In the Dark, Missing Richard Simmons, Up and Vanished

Haunted Places
Host: Greg Polcyn
Frequency: Biweekly
Average Show Length: 40 Minutes

Description:
You've heard of haunted houses, haunted cemeteries, haunted islands...but do you know how a normal place can become a paranormal minefield? Every haunted place on earth has a frightening, real backstory. Spooky legends, weird histories, and tales of the supernatural.

You May Also Like:
Creepy, Cults, Inside The Exorcist, Historical Figures, Serial Killers

Snap Judgement

Host: Glynn Washington
Frequency: Weekly
Average Show Length: 30 Minutes

Description:
Snap Judgment (Storytelling, with a BEAT) mixes real stories with killer beats to produce cinematic, dramatic, kick-ass radio. Snap's raw, musical brand of storytelling dares listeners to see the world through the eyes of another.

You May Also Like:
The Moth, Invisibilia, StoryCorps, Reply All, Embedded

Myths and Legends

Host: Jason Weiser
Frequency: Weekly
Average Show Length: 40 Minutes

Description:
Jason Weiser tells stories from myths, legends, and folklore that have shaped cultures throughout history. Some, like the stories of Aladdin, King Arthur, and Hercules are stories you think you know, but with surprising origins. Others are stories you might not have heard, but really should. All the stories are sourced from world folklore, but retold for modern ears. These are stories of wizards, knights, Vikings, dragons, princesses, and kings from the time when the world beyond the map was a dangerous and wonderful place.

You May Also Like:
Lore, Unexplained, The Black Tapes, Stuff You Missed In History Class, Casefile True Crime

The Black Tapes

Host: Alex Reagan
Frequency: Biweekly
Average Show Length: 40 Minutes

Description:

The Black Tapes is a weekly podcast from the creators of Pacific Northwest Stories, and is hosted by Alex Reagan. The Black Tapes Podcast is a serialized docudrama about one journalist's search for truth, her subject's mysterious past, and the literal and figurative ghosts that haunt them both. Do you believe?

You May Also Like:
Limetown, The NoSleep Podcast, Alice Isn't Dead, Lore, LifeAfter

Limetown
Host: Lia Haddock
Frequency: Weekly
Average Show Length: 40 Minutes
Seasoned Series (2015, 2017, 2018)

Description:
Ten years ago, over three hundred men, women and children disappeared from a small town in Tennessee, never to be heard from again. In this podcast, American Public Radio reporter Lia Haddock asks the question once more, "What happened to the people of Limetown?"

You May Also Like:
The Black Tapes, Tanis, LifeAfter, Alice Isn't Dead, Homecoming

The No Sleep Podcast
Host: David Cummings
Frequency: Weekly
Average Show Length: 90 Minutes

Description:
The NoSleep Podcast is a multi-award winning anthology series of original horror stories, with rich atmospheric music to enhance the frightening tales.

You May Also Like:
The Black Tapes, Tanis, Astonishing Legends, Unexplained, Rabbits

Magic Lessons
Host: Elizabeth Gilbert
Frequency: Weekly
Average Show Length: 60 Minutes
Seasoned Series (2016)

Description:
Bestselling author Elizabeth Gilbert hosts her hit podcast MAGIC LESSONS, ready to help another batch of aspiring artists overcome their fears and create more joyfully.

You May Also Like:
Riverhead Books, Good Life Project, The Lively Show, The Robcast, Oprah's SuperSoul Conversations

Why We Eat What We Eat
Host: Cathy Erway
Frequency: Weekly
Average Show Length: 30 Minutes

Description:
On Why We Eat What We Eat, host Cathy Erway investigates the unseen forces that shape our eating habits. We'll tackle a kale conspiracy, how to get your kids to quit being so picky, visiting the epicenter of the potluck scene, and more.

You May Also Like:
Uncivil, The Nod, Every Little Thing, The Venture, Twice Removed

The New Yorker: Fiction
Host: Deborah Treisman
Frequency: Monthly
Average Show Length: 60 Minutes

Description:
A monthly reading and conversation with the New Yorker fiction editor Deborah Treisman.

Rabbits

Host: Carly Parker
Frequency: Biweekly
Average Show Length: 60 Minutes
Seasoned Series (2017, 2018)

Description:
When Carly Parker's friend Yumiko goes missing under very mysterious circumstances, Carly's search for her friend leads her headfirst into a ancient mysterious game known only as Rabbits.

You May Also Like:
Archive 81, Darkest Night, The Bright Sessions, Limetown, Alice Isn't Dead

Tanis

Host: Nic Silver
Frequency: Biweekly
Average Show Length: 40 Minutes

Description:
Tanis is a bi-weekly podcast from the creators of Pacific Northwest Stories, and is hosted by Nic Silver. Tanis is a serialized docudrama about a fascinating and surprising mystery: the myth of Tanis. Tanis is an exploration of the nature of truth, conspiracy, and information.

You May Also Like:
Limetown, Archive 81, LifeAfter, The NoSleep Podcast, The Bright Sessions

Milk Street Radio

Host: Christopher Kimball
Frequency: Weekly
Average Show Length: 60 Minutes

Description:
This podcast asks questions and gets answers about home cooking, food, culture, wine, farming, restaurants, literature, and the lives of the people who grow, produce, and create the food we eat.

LeVar Burton Reads
Host: LeVar Burton
Frequency: Weekly
Average Show Length: 60 Minutes

Description:
Lose yourself in a great story with LeVar Burton Reads. In each episode, host LeVar Burton (Reading Rainbow, Star Trek, Roots) hand-picks a different piece of short fiction, and reads it to you.

You May Also Like:
Rabbits, Fictional, The Read, Ear Hustle, Code Switch

The Big Loop
Host: Michael Kim
Frequency: Biweekly
Average Show Length: 60 Minutes
Seasoned Series (2017)

Description:
The Big Loop is a biweekly anthology series from the co-creator of The Black Tapes. Hosted by Michael Kim, each episode is a self-contained narrative exploring the strange, the wonderful, the terrifying, and the heartbreaking.

You May Also Like:
The Black Tapes, Lore, The Unexplained, Tanis, Rabbits

The Bright Sessions
Host: Lauren Shippen
Frequency: Weekly
Average Show Length: 30 Minutes

Description:
Dr. Bright provides therapy for the strange and unusual; their sessions have been recorded for research purposes.

You May Also Like:
Archive 81, King Falls AM, The Deep Vault, Tanis, Rabbits

Sit-In
Hosts: Ally Hilfiger and Steve Hash
Frequency: Weekly
Average Show Length: 30 Minutes

Description:
Travel to the homes, studios and workplaces of the fashion world's cutting edge for a glimpse into their story, process and what drives them.

You May Also Like:
I Want Her Job, GlamMir, What's Your Jersey?, Podcast One, Wrinkled Not Dead

Alice Isn't Dead
Host: John Darnielle
Frequency: Monthly
Average Show Length: 30 Minutes
Chaptered Series (2016, 2017)

Description:
A new fiction serial from the creator of Welcome to Night Vale, Alice Isn't Dead follows a truck driver in her search across America for the wife she had long assumed was dead. In the course of her search, she will encounter not-quite-human serial murderers, towns literally lost in time, and a conspiracy that goes way beyond one missing woman.

You May Also Like:
Tanis, The Black Tapes, Limetown, Rabbits, The Bright Sessions

Bon Appétit
Host: Adam Rapoport
Frequency: Weekly
Average Show Length: 60 Minutes

Description:
The Bon Appétit Foodcast features interviews with chefs, writers, and well, anyone who has something cool to say about food.

BUSINESS

2018 Business Top Pick
Planet Money
Host: Various
Frequency: Daily
Average Show Length: 25 Minutes

The economy, explained, with stories and surprises. Imagine you could call up a friend and say, "Meet me at the bar and tell me what's going on with the economy." Now imagine that's actually a fun evening. That's what we're going for at Planet Money. People seem to like it.

You May Also Like:
Freakonomics Radio, Radiolab, Revisionist History,
99% Invisible, This American Life

How I Built This
Host: Guy Raz
Frequency: Weekly
Average Show Length: 45 Minutes

Description:
How I Built This is a podcast about innovators, entrepreneurs, and idealists, and the stories behind the movements they built. Each episode is a narrative journey marked by triumphs, failures, serendipity and insight — told by the founders of some of the world's best known companies and brands.

You May Also Like:
Revisionist History, Freakanomics Radio, The Tim Ferriss Show, 99% Invisible, The Daily

The Dave Ramsey Show
Host: Dave Ramsey
Frequency: Daily
Average Show Length: 40 Minutes

Description:
The Dave Ramsey Show is about real life and how it revolves around money. Dave Ramsey teaches you to manage and budget your money, get out of debt, build wealth, and live in financial peace. Managing your money properly will reduce stress, improve your marriage, and provide security for you and your family.

You May Also Like:
The Tony Robbins Podcast, Planet Money, The Tim Ferriss Show, Joel Osteen Podcast, The Way I Heard It with Mike Rowe

Jocko Podcast
Host: Jocko Willink
Frequency: Weekly
Average Show Length: 160 Minutes

Description:
Retired Navy SEAL, Jocko Willink and Director, Echo Charles

discuss discipline and ownership in business, war, relationships and everyday life.

You May Also Like:
The Tim Ferriss Show, The Art of Manliness, The Fighter & The Kid, Waking Up with Sam Harris, The Church of What's Happening

The Tim Ferriss Show
Host: Tim Ferriss
Frequency: Weekly
Average Show Length: 120 Minutes

Description:
Tim Ferriss is a self-experimenter and bestselling author, best known for The 4-Hour Workweek, which has been translated into 40+ languages. In this show, he deconstructs world-class performers from eclectic areas (investing, chess, pro sports, etc.), digging deep to find the tools, tactics, and tricks that listeners can use.

You May Also Like:
The Tony Robbins Podcast, How I Built This with Guy Raz, Dan Carlin's Hardcore History, The Joe Rogan Experience, Freakanomics Radio

The Tai Lopez Show
Host: Tai Lopez
Frequency: Weekly
Average Show Length: 60 Minutes

Description:
The Tai Lopez podcast brings you the best business education straight from the world's top entrepreneurs. I will also review the best books in health, wealth, love and happiness that will help you achieve your maximum potential and live the best life possible.

You May Also Like:
Cardone Zone, The GaryVee Audio Experience, The MFCEO Project, Young Hustlers, The School of Greatness with Lewis Howes

The GaryVee Audio Experience
Host: Gary Vaynerchuk
Frequency: Daily
Average Show Length: 60 Minutes

Description:
On this podcast you'll find a mix of my #AskGaryVee show episodes, keynote speeches on marketing and business, segments from my DAILYVEE video series, interviews and fireside chats I've given, as well as new and current thoughts I record originally for this audio experience!

You May Also Like:
The School of Greatness, The Tony Robbins Podcast, Entrepreneurs On Fire, Smart Passive Income, The Tim Ferriss Show

Marketing Secrets
Host: Russell Brunson
Frequency: Daily
Average Show Length: 20 Minutes

Description:
How are entrepreneurs like us, who didn't cheat and take on venture capital, who are spending money from our own wallets, how do we market in a way that lets us get our products and services and things that we believe in out to the world... and yet still remain profitable?

You May Also Like:
AMsecrets Podcast, The Caffeinated Sneakerhead, Cara Jones Speaks, No Parking, GSMC Football Podcast

Kwik Brain
Host: Jim Kwik
Frequency: Weekly
Average Show Length: 15 Minutes

Description:
A fun, fast-paced show designed to help busy people learn and achieve anything in a fraction of the time!

Rebel Traders
Hosts: Sean Donahoe, Phil Newton
Frequency: Weekly
Average Show Length: 90 Minutes

Description:
Inside the world of two underground master traders who take an entertaining, unique and often contrarian look at the markets and business. Cutting through the noise of Wall Street shenanigans and hijinks and the clutter and confusion of mainstream news, they are here to help you navigate the trading minefield so you can finally take control of your financial future.

You May Also Like:
Lifestyle Trading 101, Real Traders Webinar, Charting Wealth, Let's Talk Stocks, Stock Market Mentor Chart of the Day

Ted Talks Business
Host: Various
Frequency: Weekly
Average Show Length: 15 Minutes

Description:
Some of the world's greatest innovators, entrepreneurs, and business researchers share their stories and insights from the stage at TED conferences and TEDx events around the world.

You May Also Like:
HBR IdeaCast, The Tony Robbins Podcast, We Study Billionaires, The Economist Radio, The Tim Ferriss Show

Business & Biceps
Hosts: Cory Gregor, John Fosco
Frequency: Daily
Average Show Length: 45 Minutes

Description:
Insights that are sure to make you stronger in business and in the gym.

LinkedIn's Work In Progress
Host: Caroline Fairchild
Frequency: Weekly
Average Show Length: 30 Minutes

Description:
Work. It's what we do. It's how we survive. And, for many, it's who we are. The question: Where's it headed? Work In Progress, hosted by LinkedIn Senior Editor Caroline Fairchild, dives into the fascinating world of work now, featuring discussions with some of the economy's brightest thinkers and on-the-ground interviews with workers around the U.S., all grappling with change.

You May Also Like:
21st Century Entrepreneurship, Beyond the States, Tony Central Podcast, Cafecito Bros, Expect Success

BiggerPockets Podcast
Hosts: Josh Dorkin, Brandon Turner
Frequency: Weekly
Average Show Length: 90 Minutes

Description:
Imagine you are friends with hundreds of real estate investors and entrepreneurs. Now imagine you can grab a beer with each of them and casually chat about failures, successes, motivations, and lessons learned. That's what The BiggerPockets Podcast delivers. Co-hosted by BiggerPockets' founder and CEO Joshua Dorkin and active real estate investor Brandon Turner, this podcast provides actionable advice from investors and other real estate professionals every week. The show won't tell you how to "get rich quick" or sell you a course, boot camp, or guru system; instead, the BiggerPockets Podcast will give you real strategies that work for real people.

You May Also Like:
Lifetime Cash Flow Through Real Estate Investing, The Real Estate Guys, We Study Billionaires, The Rich Dad Radio Show, Smart Passive Income

Masters of Scale
Host: Reid Hoffman
Frequency: Weekly
Average Show Length: 30 Minutes

Description:
How do companies grow from zero to a gazillion? Legendary Silicon Valley investor / entrepreneur Reid Hoffman tests his theories with famous founders.

You May Also Like:
A16z, The Pitch, StartUp Podcast, Recode Decode, How I Built This

Optimal Finance Daily
Host: Various
Frequency: Daily
Average Show Length: 10 Minutes

Description:
Optimal Finance Daily is a podcast created for those looking to improve their financial lives one step at a time: lifelong learners and life optimizers. We bring you the best content from blogs and other resources and read it to you, so that you don't have to waste your time finding and reading blogs yourself--listen during your commute, workout, regular routines, or during your down time 7 days a week and improve your life one step at a time.

You May Also Like:
Radical Personal Finance, Money For The Rest of Us, Listen Money Matters, Stacking Benjamins, Financial Independance

The Indicator
Host: Stacy Smith, Cardiff Garcia
Frequency: Daily
Average Show Length: 10 Minutes

The Indicator helps you make sense of what's happening today. It's a quick hit of insight into work, business, the economy, and everything else.

The Brutal Truth About Sales & Selling
Host: Brian Burns
Frequency: Weekly
Average Show Length: 45 Minutes

Description:
If are selling or in sales this podcast is for you. Some of the topics covered are cold calling, spin selling, challenger sale, solution selling, advanced selling skills. strategic selling, linkedin, saas, sales leadership, sales management, social media, b2b marketing, maverick selling method and how sales has changed.

You May Also Like:
The B2B Revenue Leadership Show, Sips Suds and Smokes, Stand Up Speak Up, Flipping Houses for Rookies, Are You Real

Marketplace
Host: Kai Ryssdal
Frequency: Weekly
Average Show Length: 25 Minutes

Description:
Clear explorations of how economic news affects you, through stories, conversations, newsworthy numbers and more. Airing each weekday evening on your local public radio station or on-demand anytime, Marketplace is your liaison between economics and life.

You May Also Like:
Motley Fool Money, Masters in Business, Exchanges at Goldman Sachs, On the Media, HBR IdeaCast

Impact Theory
Host: Tom Bilyeu
Frequency: Daily
Average Show Length: 60 Minutes

Description:
Impact Theory is a business and mindset-focused interview show that will teach anyone aspiring to greatness the secrets to success.

The MFCEO Project
Host: Andy Frisella
Frequency: Weekly
Average Show Length: 20 Minutes

Description:
The MFCEO Project is for anyone who is sick of the fluffy unicorns and rainbows style of talking about pursuing goals and profiting in business. In this podcast, Andy Frisella (and his guests) share insights on success and failure, in straight up fashion.

You May Also Like:
Cardone Zone, The GaryVee Audio Experience, Self Made Man, Order of Man, The Tai Lopez Show

Hacking Your Leadership
Hosts: Chris Stark & Lorenzo Flores
Frequency: Biweekly
Average Show Length: 20 Minutes

Description:
No role plays; just real. Chris & Lorenzo share four decades of combined experience to help you become a more effective leader. New episodes every Monday and Thursday.

You May Also Like:
3 People Like This, Dr. Lars Dingman, The Caffeinated Sneakerhead, Crossroads of Health, Why I'm Not...

From 7 To 8 Figures
Host: Trevor Chapman
Frequency: Daily
Average Show Length: 30 Minutes

Description:
Everything necessary to become a 7-figure and 8-figure entrepreneur.

Girlboss Radio
Host: Sophia Amoruso
Frequency: Weekly
Average Show Length: 50 Minutes

Description:
Sophia interviews boundary-pushing women who've made their mark—eschewing polite conversation and extracting solid advice from the lessons they've learned along the way. Expect hilarious co-hosts and vulnerable, honest conversations you won't hear anywhere else. Conversations that humanize the known, champion the unknown, and laugh a little at the absurdity of life.

You May Also Like:
Women of The Hour, The Lively Show, Call Your Girlfriend, Dear Sugars, Magic Lessons

The B2B Revenue Leadership Show
Host: Brian Burns
Frequency: Weekly
Average Show Length: 30 Minutes

Description:
This podcast is focused on leadership in the B2B space to drive revenue by using the most modern and scientific approaches. If you are a CEO, VC, CRO, CMO or want to be one some day this podcast is for you.

You May Also Like:
Stand Up Speak Up, Casual Friday, Jim Beaver's Project Action, Sips, Suds, & Smokes, The Down & Dirty Radio Show

Crypto 101
Host: Matthew Aaron
Frequency: Daily
Average Show Length: 30 Minutes

Description:
The Average Consumers Guide to Cryptocurrency.

Side Hustle School
Host: Chris Guillebeau
Frequency: Daily
Average Show Length: 10 Minutes

Description:
In each episode, listeners will hear a different story of someone who's started a side hustle—along with what went well, how that person overcame challenges, and what happened as a result.

You May Also Like:
The Side Hustle Show, Smart Passive Income, Good Life Project, Don't Keep Your Day Job, The Minimalists

More Than Money
Host: Dawn Carpenter
Frequency: Monthly
Average Show Length: 30 Minutes
Seasoned Series (2017)

Description:
A conversation community around how to use your values to engage with work and invest your wealth. In this podcast, we explore the following topic areas: (1) business ethics, (2) economic justice, (3) corporate social responsibility, (4) social entrepreneurship, (5) community development, and (6) faith and values-based investing.

You May Also Like:
Choppin' It Up, Nerds With Words, Are You Hearing This!, Loud Americans Discuss Soccer, Inappropriate Earl

Funny Money
Hosts: Bob Wheeler, Sheldon Anderson
Frequency: Weekly
Average Show Length: 30 Minutes

Description:
Weekly podcast covering money, finances, and investing.

WSJ What's News
Host: Various
Frequency: Daily
Average Show Length: 10 Minutes

Description:
Top stories. Timely insights. From business and markets to politics and breaking news, stay informed on the news you need to know throughout your day with WSJ journalists and notable influencers.

You May Also Like:
FT News, Bloomberg Surveillance, Masters in Business, Exchanges at Goldman Sachs, The Economist: The Week Ahead

We Study Billionaires
Host: Preston Psyh and Stig Brodersen
Frequency: Weekly
Average Show Length: 50 Minutes

Description:
We like to have fun and study billionaires. We interview entrepreneurs and highly influential authors of business books.

You May Also Like:
Masters In Business, Bigger Pockets Podcast, Smart Passive Income, Motley Fool Money, Rich Dad Radio Show

Fintech Insider
Hosts: David Brear, Jason Bates, Chris Skinner, Simon Taylor
Frequency: Daily
Average Show Length: 60 Minutes

Description:
FinTech Insider Interviews brings you one-on-one interviews with the thought leaders and innovators transforming financial services.

You May Also Like:
Stand Up Speak Up, Jim Beaver's Project Action, Casual Friday, Sips, Suds, & Smokes, The B2B Revenue Leadership Show

HBR IdeaCast
Host: Sarah Green Carmichael
Frequency: Weekly
Average Show Length: 20 Minutes

Description:
A weekly podcast featuring the leading thinkers in business and management from Harvard Business Review.

You May Also Like:
The McKinsey Podcast, TEDTalks Business, The Economist Radio, Entrepreneurial Thought Leaders, We Study Billionaires

Smart Passive Income
Host: Pat Flynn
Frequency: Weekly
Average Show Length: 60 Minutes

Description:
Online business and blogging strategies, income sources and killer marketing tips and tricks so you can be ahead of the curve with your online business or blog. .

You May Also Like:
Entrepreneurs On Fire, Online Marketing Made Easy, The School of Greatness, This Is Your Life, Social Media Marketing Podcast

StartUp Podcast
Host: Alex Blumberg
Frequency: Weekly
Average Show Length: 30 Minutes
Seasoned Series (2014, 2015, 2016, 2017)

Description:
A series about what it's really like to start a business.

You May Also Like:
How I Built This, Planet Money, Masters of Scale, 99% Invisible, Death, Sex & Money

COMEDY

2018 Comedy Top Pick
Joe Rogan Experience
Host: Joe Rogan
Frequency: Daily
Average Show Length: 180 Minutes

The podcast of comedian and UFC
commentator Joe Rogan.

You May Also Like:
Monday Morning Podcast, Dan Carlin's Hardcore
History, The Tim Ferriss Show, Stuff You Should Know,
WTF with Marc Maron

My Favorite Murder
Hosts: Karen Kilgariff and Georgia Hardstark
Frequency: Weekly
Average Show Length: 120 Minutes

Description:
Lifelong fans of true crime stories Karen Kilgariff and Georgia Hardstark tell each other their favorite tales of murder and hear hometown crime stories from friends and fans.

You May Also Like:
Last Podcast On The Left, Sword and Scale, Casefile True Crime, Up and Vanished, Lore

The Daily Zeitgeist
Host: Jack O'Brien
Frequency: Daily
Average Show Length: 60 Minutes

Description:
Lifelong fans of true crime stories Karen Kilgariff and Georgia Hardstark tell each other their favorite tales of murder and hear hometown crime stories from friends and fans.

You May Also Like:
Cracked Gets Personal, Kurt Vonneguys, Cracked Movie Club, Unpopular Opinion, Buzzfeed News

My Dad Wrote A Porno
Host: Jamie Morton
Frequency: Weekly
Average Show Length: 45 Minutes

Description:
Imagine if your Dad wrote a dirty book. Most people would try to ignore it and pretend it had never happened - but not Jamie Morton. Instead, he's decided to read it to the world in this brand new comedy podcast. With the help of his friends, James Cooper and BBC Radio 1's Alice Levine, Jamie will be reading a chapter a week

and discovering more about his father than he ever bargained for.

You May Also Like:
No Such Thing As A Fish, S-Town, My Favorite Murder, Casefile True Crime,

The Pat McAfee Show
Host: Pat McAfee
Frequency: Biweekly
Average Show Length: 90 Minutes

Description:
On "The Pat McAfee Show" Pat McAfee and his friends deliver one of a kind opinions that won't be heard anywhere else. Pat's a recently retired NFL All Pro who has zero filter. A common man who has experience in an extremely uncommon professional athlete lifestyle is a beautiful concoction of hilarity for the average Joe. Both relatable and ridiculous, "The Pat McAfee Show" promises to inform, intrigue, and entertain at least twice a week.

You May Also Like:
The Dave Portnoy Show, Barstool Rundown, Young & Happy, Pardon My Take, Fore Play

Raised by TV
Hosts: Job Gabrus, Lauren Lapkus
Frequency: Weekly
Average Show Length: 60 Minutes

Description:
Two former latchkey kid sisters reveal their unhealthy obsession with television by discussing their overly passionate feelings about a different show each episode.

You May Also Like:
Julian Loves Music, High and Mighty, Doughboys, The Pod F. Tompkast, View from the Cheap Seats

Wait Wait... Don't Tell Me!
Host: Peter Sagal
Frequency: Weekly
Average Show Length: 50 Minutes

Description:
NPR's weekly current events quiz. Have a laugh and test your news knowledge while figuring out what's real and what we've made up.

You May Also Like:
The Moth, Radiolab, This American Life, Freakanomics Radio

WTF with Marc Maron
Host: Marc Maron
Frequency: Weekly
Average Show Length: 90 Minutes

Description:
Comedian Marc Maron is tackling the most complex philosophical question of our day - WTF? He'll get to the bottom of it with help from comedian friends, celebrity guests and the voices in his own head.

You May Also Like:
The Nerdist, Monday Morning Podcast, Fresh Air, Radiolab, Dan Carlin's Hardcore History

2 Dope Queens
Hosts: Phoebe Robinson and Jessica Williams
Frequency: Weekly
Average Show Length: 50 Minutes

Description:
Join the 2 Dope Queens, along with their favorite comedians, for stories about sex, romance, race, hair journeys, living in New York, and Billy Joel.

You May Also Like:
Code Switch, Another Round, The Read, Invisibilia, Modern Love

Last Podcast On The Left
Hosts: Ben Kissel, Marcus Parks, Henry Zebrowski
Frequency: Weekly
Average Show Length: 90 Minutes

Description:
The Last Podcast On The Left covers all the horrors our world has to offer both imagined and real, from demons and slashers to cults and serial killers, The Last Podcast is guaranteed to satisfy your bloodlust.

You May Also Like:
My Favorite Murder, Sword and Scale, True Crime Garage, Someone Knows Something, Casefile True Crime

Bill Burr's Monday Morning Podcast
Host: Bill Burr
Frequency: Biweekly
Average Show Length: 90 Minutes

Description:
Bill Burr rants about relationship advice, sports and the Illuminati.

You May Also Like:
The Joe Rogan Experience, WTF, The Church of What's Happening, Dan Carlin's Hardcore History, The Nerdist

Anna Faris Is Unqualified
Host: Anna Faris
Frequency: Weekly
Average Show Length: 60 Minutes

Description:
Not-great-relationship advice from completely unqualified Hollywood types.

You May Also Like:
*My Favorite Murder, Guys We F****d, 2 Dope Queens, The Nerdist, Women of the Hour*

The Breakfast Club
Hosts: DJ Envy, Angela Yee, Charlamagne Tha God
Frequency: Biweekly
Average Show Length: 60 Minutes

Description:
The world's most dangerous morning show.

You May Also Like:
Angela Yee's Lip Service, The Joe Budden Podcast, On One with Angela Rye, The Brilliant Idiots, Drink Champs

Guys We F****d
Hosts: Corinne Fisher, Krystyna Hutchinson
Frequency: Weekly
Average Show Length: 120 Minutes

Description:
They spread their legs, now they're spreading the word that women should be able to have sex with WHOEVER they want WHENEVER they want and not be ashamed or called sluts or whores. Welcome to a new revolution. Each week, Corinne Fisher & Krystyna Hutchinson (together known as the comedy duo Sorry About Last Night) interview a gentleman they slept with. Some they made love to, some they had sex with a few times and some they f****d in a hotel bathroom...er, what?

You May Also Like:
Anna Faris Is Unqualified, 2 Dope Queens, My Favorite Murder, Modern Love, Women of the Hour

KFC Radio
Hosts: Tyler Oakley, Korey Kuhl
Frequency: Biweekly
Average Show Length: 45 Minutes

Description:
Featuring all of the regular Barstool personalities, KFC Radio is the quintessential bar conversation brought to podcast form. Listener

interaction is the name of the game as Barstool readers and listeners contribute their Stoolie Voicemails to drive the conversation to strange places including embarrassing personal stories, bizarre hypothetical questions, and more.

You May Also Like:
The Dave Portnoy Show, Barstool Rundown, Young & Happy, Pardon My Take, Fore Play

Shane and Friends
Host: Shane Dawson
Frequency: Weekly
Average Show Length: 60 Minutes

Description:
I'm Shane Dawson and I have a lot of friends. Most of them are in my head. Listen as me and my producer Lauren Schnipper talk about stuff we think is funny and interview people we hope are funny. Also I like to do character voices and celebrity impressions but I promise, it's not as annoying as it sounds.

You May Also Like:
Jenna & Julien Podcast, Views, Not Too Deep, Psychobabble, Ear Biscuits

The Dollop
Host: Dave Anthony, Gareth Reynolds
Frequency: Weekly
Average Show Length: 90 Minutes

Description:
Comedians Dave Anthony and Gareth Reynolds pick a subject from history and examine it.

You May Also Like:
Last Podcast on the Left, My Favorite Murder, Dumb People Town, True Crime Garage, You Must Remember

The Nerdist
Host: Chris Hardwick
Frequency: Biweekly
Average Show Length: 90 Minutes

Description:
This podcast is basically just me talking about stuff and things with my two nerdy friends Jonah Ray and Matt Mira, and usually someone more famous than all of us. Occasionally we swear because that is fun.

You May Also Like:
WTF, StarTalk Radio, How Did This Get Made, Monday Morning Podcast

Welcome to Night Vale
Host: Cecil Baldwin
Frequency: Biweekly
Average Show Length: 30 Minutes

Description:
Twice-monthly community updates for the small desert town of Night Vale, featuring local weather, news, announcements from the Sheriff's Secret Police, mysterious lights in the night sky, dark hooded figures with unknowable powers, and cultural events. Turn on your radio and hide. Never listened before? It's an ongoing radio show. Start with the current episode, and you'll catch on in no time.

You May Also Like:
Lore, The Black Tapes, Limetown, Myths and Legends, Tanis

The Read
Host: Kid Fury, Crissle
Frequency: Bi-Weekly
Average Show Length: 30 Minutes

Description:
Join bloggers Kid Fury and Crissle for their weekly "read" of hip-hop and pop culture's most trying stars. Throwing shade and spilling

tea with a flippant and humorous attitude, no star is safe from Fury and Crissle unless their name is Beyonce. Or Blue Ivy. As recent transplants to New York City (Fury from Miami and Crissle from Oklahoma City), The Read also serves as an on air therapy session for two friends trying to adjust to life (and rats) in the big city.

You May Also Like:
Another Round, 2 Dope Queens, Bodega Boys, Black Girls Talking, Code Switch

How Did This Get Made
Hosts: Paul Scheer, June Diane Raphael, Jason Mantzoukas
Frequency: Weekly
Average Show Length: 90 Minutes

Description:
Have you ever seen a movie so bad that it's amazing? Paul Scheer ('The League'), June Diane Raphael (Netflix's 'Grace and Frankie'), and Jason Mantzoukas ('Kroll Show') watch them with their funniest friends, then get down to the fundamental question: How Did This Get Made?

You May Also Like:
Doug Loves Movies, You Made It Weird, The Nerdist, WTF with Marc Maron

The Church of What's Happneing Now
Host: Joey "Coco" Diaz
Frequency: Daily
Average Show Length: 90 Minutes

Description:
What's Happening Now With: Joey Coco Diaz is a twice-weekly podcast hosted by Comedian Joey Coco Diaz along with his co-host Lee Syatt. Joey doesn't hold anything back and let's you know exactly what's on his mind. Joey and Lee are joined by one of Joey's friends, Comedians, Actors, Writers and Director's to name a few. We look forward to having you as a member of The Church.

EDUCATION

2018 Education Top Pick
Tony Robbins Podcast
Host: Tony Robbins
Frequency: Weekly
Average Show Length: 50 Minutes

Tony Robbins, the #1 Life and Business Strategist, has helped over 50 million people from 100 countries create real and lasting change in their lives. In this podcast, he shares proven strategies and tactics so you, too, can achieve massive results in your business, relationships, health and finances.

You May Also Like:
The Tim Ferriss Show, The School of Greatness with Lewis Howes, The GaryVee Audio Experience, Flipping Houses for Rookies

Duolingo Spanish Podcast – Duolingo
Host: Martina Castro
Frequency: Seasonal
Average Show Length: 15 Minutes

Description:
True stories for English speakers learning Spanish. From the makers of Duolingo, the most popular language-learning app, comes a new podcast that delivers fascinating real-life stories in easy-to-understand Spanish with English narration. These are not language lessons; they're life lessons through language. Hosted by Martina Castro, co-founder of NPR's Radio Ambulante.

You May Also Like:
Stuff You Missed in History Class, S-Town, This American Life

Flipping Houses for Rookies
Host: Various
Frequency: Weekly
Average Show Length: 60 Minutes

Description:
"Discover the secret methods I'm using to earn massive piles of cash By "flipping houses" without using my own money or credit! This method works in ANY economy, in any geographic location, and can be done by anyone, regardless of their credit or finances. Is it possible to earn a six-figure income on a part time schedule? Find out what my students and I are doing without using our own money or credit to flip real estate! If you are looking to increase your income, or just simply take in huge extra chunks of cash, without working 80 hours per week, you are in the right place. What you will discover here and nowhere else on the Internet is a systematic and simple training system that anyone can implement to make money investing in real estate.

You May Also Like:
Sips, Suds, & Smokes, Thaddeus Ellenburg's Casual Friday, Jim Beaver's Project Action

The Art of Charm
Host: Jordan Harbinger
Frequency: Daily
Average Show Length: 60 Minutes

Description:
Social science, behavioral economics, cognitive psychology -- sound complex? Let's fix that. The Art of Charm Podcast is where self-motivated guys and gals, just like you, come to learn from a diverse mix of experienced mentors, including the world's best professional and academic minds, scientists, innovators, coaches, relationship experts, entrepreneurs, bestselling authors, and other brilliant minds. This show will make you a higher performer, a better networker, a deeper connector and, most importantly, a better thinker.

You May Also Like:
The Art of Manliness, The School of Greatness with Lewis Howes, The Tim Ferriss Show

Kwik Brain
Host: Jim Kwik
Frequency: Weekly
Average Show Length: 15 Minutes

Description:
In this easy to digest bite-sized podcast, you will discover Kwik's favorite shortcuts to read faster, remember more, and 'supercharge' your greatest wealth-building asset: your brain. Whether you're a student, senior, entrepreneur or educator, you will get the edge with these simple actionable tools to sharpen your mind, enhance your focus, and fast-track your fullest potential.

You May Also Like:
Impact Theory with Tom Bilyeu, The Model Health Show, The James Altucher Show

The Jordan B. Peterson Podcast
Host: Dr. Jordan B. Peterson
Frequency: Weekly
Average Show Length: 90 Minutes

Description:
This podcast is a collection of interviews & lectures, some of which are recorded specifically for this podcast, and some that are from his university courses, public lectures, documentary interviews, and YouTube videos from his channel: Jordan Peterson Videos (https://www.youtube.com/user/JordanPetersonVideos). The podcast offers discussion and information concerning a variety of complex ideas: How moral & pragmatic values regulate emotion and motivation; Psychometric models such as the Big Five; The significance of hero mythology; The meaning of music, and the structure of the world as represented through religion and spiritual belief.

You May Also Like:
The Rubin Report, Freedomain Radio with Stefan Molyneux, Louder With Crowder

Coffee Break Spanish
Host: Mark Pentleton
Frequency: Monthly
Average Show Length: 60 Minutes

Description:
Learn Spanish in coffee-break lessons from the Radio Lingua Network. In each lesson we'll focus on the language you need to know and before long you'll be making yourself understood with native Spanish speakers. Season 1 lessons are for absolute beginners, and the courses increase in difficulty as the seasons progress.

You May Also Like:
Learn Spanish - Survival Guide, Spanish Podcast, Learn to Speak Spanish with Discover Spanish

Impact Theory with Tom Bilyeu
Host: Tom Bilyeu
Frequency: Daily
Average Show Length: 15 Minutes

Description:
Impact Theory is a business and mindset-focused interview show that will teach anyone aspiring to greatness the secrets to success. The show is hosted by Tom Bilyeu - a serial entrepreneur and co-founder of the #2 Inc. 500 company Quest Nutrition and former host of the viral hit Youtube series Inside Quest (viewed over 100,000,000 times). Bilyeu is known for his passion and preparation. Always eager to truly learn from his guests, Bilyeu digs deep and brings the urgency of someone hungry to put what he's learning to immediate use - making the show not only entertaining and energetic, but also hyper-useful.

You May Also Like:
Kwik Brain, The Unbeatable Mind Podcast with Mark Divine, London Real

Coffee Break French – Radio Lingua Network
Host: Mark Pentleton
Frequency: Monthly
Average Show Length: 15 Minutes

Description:
Learn French in coffee-break lessons from the Radio Lingua Network. In each lesson we'll focus on the language you need to know and before long you'll be making yourself understood with native French speakers. Season 1 lessons are for absolute beginners, and the courses increase in difficulty as the seasons progress.

You May Also Like:
Learn French by Podcast, French Podcast, French for Beginners

TEDTalks Education – TED Conferences LLC
Host: Various
Frequency: Monthly
Average Show Length: 15 Minutes

Description:
What should future schools look like? How do brains learn? Some of the world's greatest educators, researchers, and community leaders share their stories and visions onstage at the TED conference, TEDx events and partner events around the world. You can also download these and many other videos free on TED.com, with an interactive English transcript and subtitles in up to 80 languages. TED is a nonprofit devoted to Ideas Worth Spreading.

You May Also Like:
K-12 Greatest Hits:The Best Ideas in Education, Grammar Girl Quick and Dirty Tips for Better Writing, The Cult of Pedagogy Podcast

The Majority Report with Sam Seder
Host: Sam Seder
Frequency: Daily
Average Show Length: 60 Minutes

Description:
Entertaining Daily Politics, Award Winning Long-Form Interviews and Irreverent, Independent Analysis.

You May Also Like:
Ring of Fire Radio with Sam Seder, The David Pakman Show, The Jimmy Dore Show

Grammar Girl Quick and Dirty Tips for Better Writing
Host: Mignon Fogarty
Frequency: Weekly
Average Show Length: 15 minutes

Description:
Grammar Girl provides short, friendly tips to improve your writing. Whether English is your first language or your second language,

these grammar, punctuation, style, and business tips will make you a better and more successful writer. Grammar Girl is a Quick and Dirty Tips podcast.

You May Also Like:
How To Do Everything, Stuff Mom Never Told You, The Art of Charm

Learn Spanish - Survival Guide
Host: David Spencer
Frequency: Weekly
Average Show Length: 15 Minutes

Description:
This podcast is about learning to speak Spanish in every day practical situations. There are pauses for you to repeat what you hear and the more difficult words and phrases are broken down for correct pronunciation and grammar. There are songs, games and other activities to make your learning enjoyable and help you retain what you have learned. We are the first podcast using this style of teaching, and with a state certified professional Spanish teacher, you know you're in good hands. So subscribe today and get started with your learning.

You May Also Like:
Learn to Speak Spanish with Discover Spanish, Coffee Break Spanish

EconTalk
Host: Russ Roberts
Frequency: Weekly
Average Show Length: 60 Minutes

Description:
EconTalk is an award-winning weekly talk show about economics in daily life.

You May Also Like:
LSE: Public lectures and events, Masters in Business, Intelligence Squared U.S. Debates

Learn French With Daily Podcasts
Host: Various
Frequency: Daily
Average Show Length: 7 minutes

Description:
Learn French with free daily podcasts, brought to you by French teachers from Paris. DailyFrenchPod is an amazing effective and new way to learn French.

You May Also Like:
Learn French by Podcast, Coffee Break French, French for Beginners

Every Little Thing
Host: Flora Lichtman
Frequency: Weekly
Average Show Length: 30 Minutes

Description:
Turn over the rock, peek through the keyhole, go down the rabbit hole. There's always more to it. A new show from Gimlet Media, hosted by Flora Lichtman.

You May Also Like:
Undiscovered, Open For Business, Rough Translation

Slate Presents Lexicon Valley
Host: John H. McWhorter
Frequency: Weekly
Average Show Length: 30 Minutes

Description:
Lexicon Valley is a podcast about language, from pet peeves, syntax, and etymology to neurolinguistics and the death of languages.

You May Also Like:
A Way with Words, The History of English Podcast, The Allusionist

Spanish Podcast
Host: Various
Frequency: Weekly
Average Show Length: 8 Minutes

Description:
News in Slow Spanish is a podcast for those who already possess a basic vocabulary and some knowledge of Spanish grammar. Your host are native Spanish speaker from Spain. In our program we discuss the world news, grammar, and expressions, and much more in simplified Spanish at a slow pace so that you can understand almost every word and sentence. Learn real Spanish with us! In our course we emphasize all aspects of language learning from listening comprehension, rapid vocabulary expansion, exposure to grammar and common idiomatic expressions, to pronunciation practice and interactive grammar exercises.

You May Also Like:
Latin American Spanish, Notes in Spanish Intermediate, Learn Spanish: Notes in Spanish Inspired Beginners

Optimal Living Daily
Host: Joc Marie
Frequency: Daily
Average Show Length: 10 Minutes

Description:
Optimal Living Daily is a podcast created for those looking to improve their life one step at a time: lifelong learners, life hackers, and life optimizers. Joc Marie brings you the best content from blogs and other resources and reads it to you, so that you don't have to waste your time finding and reading blogs yourself--listen during your commute, workout, regular routines, or during your down time 7 days a week and improve your life one step at a time.

You May Also Like:
Optimal Living Daily The Scott Alan Turner Show , Relationships, Sex, Dating and Marriage Advice - I Do Podcast

The Business of Fashion Podcast
Host: The Business of Fashion
Frequency: Weekly
Average Show Length: 30 Minutes

Description:
The Business of Fashion has gained a global following as an essential daily resource for fashion creatives, executives and entrepreneurs in over 200 countries. It is frequently described as "indispensable," "required reading" and "an addiction."

You May Also Like:
Fashion No Filter, Fashion Is Your Business - a retail technology podcast, The Glossy Podcast

The Cult of Pedagogy Podcast
Host: Jennifer Gonzalez
Frequency: Weekly
Average Show Length: 60 Minutes

Description:
Jennifer Gonzalez interviews educators, students, administrators and parents about the psychological and social dynamics of school, trade secrets, and other juicy things you'll never learn in a textbook.

You May Also Like:
Talks with Teachers, Every Classroom Matters With Cool Cat Teacher, K-12 Greatest Hits:The Best Ideas in Education

English as a Second Language (ESL) Podcast
Host: Jeff McQuillan
Frequency: Seasonal
Average Show Length: 30 minutes

Description:
Improve English speaking and listening skills.

You May Also Like:
6 Minute English, The English We Speak, All Ears English Podcast

All Ears English Podcast
Host: Lindsay McMahon, Michelle Kaplan
Frequency: Daily
Average Show Length: 20 Minutes

Description:
Are you looking for a new and fun way to learn American English?
Come hang out with Lindsay and Michelle from Boston and New
York City and have fun while you improve your English listening
skills! All Ears English is an English as a Second Language (ESL)
podcast for intermediate to advanced English learners around the
world. Teachers Lindsay McMahon and Michelle Kaplan will show
you how to use everyday English vocabulary and natural idioms,
expressions, and phrasal verbs and how to make small talk in
American English. We will also give you special tips on American
culture, customs, etiquette, and how to speak with Americans as well
as conversation and commentary on study tips, business English, life
in America and Boston and New York.

You May Also Like:
*English as a Second Language (ESL) Podcast, The English We
Speak, All Ears English Podcast*

Latin American Spanish – Linguistica 360
Host: Linguistica 360
Frequency: Weekly
Average Show Length: 10 Minutes

Description:
In our course we emphasize all aspects of language learning from
listening comprehension, rapid vocabulary expansion, exposure
to Spanish grammar and common idiomatic expressions used in
Latin America, to pronunciation practice and interactive grammar
exercises. In our program we discuss the Weekly News, grammar,
and expressions, and much more in simplified Spanish at a slow
pace so that you can understand almost every word and sentence.

You May Also Like:
Spanish Podcast, Notes in Spanish Intermediate

GAMES & HOBBIES

2018 Games & Hobbies Top Pick
Critical Role
Host: Matthew Mercer
Frequency: Daily
Average Show Length: 180 Minutes

Voice actor Matthew Mercer leads a group of fellow voice actors on epic Dungeons & Dragons campaigns. These familiar voices bring the audience into the full experience of D&D, allowing imaginations to soar as the characters embark on adventures. This is Critical Role!

You May Also Like:
Drunks and Dragons - Dungeons and Dragons 5e Actual Play, Dungeon Delve – An Official Dungeons & Dragons Podcast, allworknoplay, Dragon Talk - An Official Dungeons & Dragons Podcast, Critical Hit: A Dungeons and Dragons Campaign

Car Talk
Hosts: Tom Magliozz, Ray Magliozzi
Frequency: Weekly
Average Show Length:50 Minutes

Description:
America's funniest auto mechanics take calls from weary car owners all over the country, and crack wise while they diagnose Dodges and dismiss Diahatsus.

You May Also Like:
Science Friday, A Prairie Home Companion, Snap Judgment, The Way I Heard It, The Moth

Skidmarks Show
Host: Jeff Allen & Ethan D.
Frequency: Weekly
Average Show Length: 60 Minutes

Description:
SkidMarks Show is based on cool cars and rock stars all in the vein of comedy, a true light hearted approach with guests from race car drivers, rock and roll legends and celebrities.

You May Also Like:
GSMC MMA Podcast, GSMC Fantasy Football Podcast, GSMC Women's MMA Podcast, Cara Jones Speaks.

Game Scoop!
Hosts: Daemon Hatfield, Justin Davis
Frequency: Weekly
Average Show Length: 90 Minutes

Description:
IGN shoots a week's worth of gaming news straight into your ear!

You May Also Like:
Kinda Funny Gamescast, PS I Love You XOXO, Giant Bombcast, The GameOverGreggy Show, The Game Informer Show

Giant Bombcast
Host: Various
Frequency: Weekly
Average Show Length: 120 Minutes

Description:
Giant Bomb discusses the latest video game news and new releases, taste-test questionable beverages, and get wildly off-topic in this weekly podcast.

You May Also Like:
The Giant Beastcastm,Podcast Beyond, PS I Love You XOXO,Giant Bomb Presents, Kinda Funny Gamescast

Dragons In Places
Host: Game Grumps
Frequency: Weekly
Average Show Length: 60 Minutes

Description:
Dragons in Places is a Dungeons and Dragons podcast by Game Grumps.

You May Also Like:
The G Club, Before the Grumps,SuperMegaCast, Schmucks Podcast , Heroes & Halfwits.

Star Wars: New Canon Book Club
Host: Jesse Cox
Frequency: Weekly
Average Show Length: 90 Minutes

Description:
Three friends gather to talk about the newest Star Wars books with the world.

You May Also Like:
Cox n' Crendor Show, The Co-optional Podcast, Full Of Sith: Star Wars News, Star Wars: Beyond the Films

Brute Force
Host: Adam Bash
Frequency: Weekly
Average Show Length: 60 Minutes

Description:
Brute Force is a real-play comedic RPG podcast blended with in-character narration. We play a campaign of FATE Core (we started with World of Darkness) set in the high fantasy world of Eorith. The adventurers are a party of monsters tasked with saving a world that barely tolerates their existence.

You May Also Like:
Cthulhu & Friends, Fistful of Pixels, GeeklyInc: Random Encounters, Cthulhu & Friends Presents: Side Quests, The Abridged Drunks and Dragons

Dude Soup
Host: Various
Frequency: Weekly
Average Show Length: 60 Minutes

Description:
Jump in the Dude Soup -- all the gaming, nerd culture, and meat-packing industry commentary you can handle.

You May Also Like:
Internet Box, PS I Love You XOXO, Giant Bombcast, Kinda Funny Gamescast, The GameOverGreggy Show.

Good Job, Brain!
Host: Karen Chu, Colin Felton, Dana Nelson and Chris Kohler
Frequency: Weekly
Average Show Length: 60 Minutes

Description:
Part pub quiz show, part offbeat news, and all awesome. All the time! We here are nuts about trivia. And we are darn sure there are people out there who share our unusual obsession. Do you relish

beating your friends at Trivial Pursuit? Do you blab out the answers at the gym when Jeopardy! is on? Then this podcast, fellow trivia nut, is the ultimate mental nutrition for your very big brain. So eat up!

You May Also Like:
The Comedy Button, The Podcast History Of Our World, Ask Me Another, A Way with Words, The Geekbox

Podcast Beyond
Host: Various
Frequency: Weekly
Average Show Length: 60 Minutes

Description:
The IGN PlayStation Team sits down and talks all things Sony, sprinkling a little madness and song along the way. Podcast Beyond is the premiere source for Sony news, opinions and old-fashioned shenanigans.

You May Also Like:
PS I Love You XOXO, Giant Bombcast, Kinda Funny Gamescast, The GameOverGreggy Show, Kinda Funny Games Daily

Car Stuff
Hosts: Ben Bowlin and Scott Benjamin
Frequency: Weekly
Average Show Length: 90 Minutes

Description:
What's the history of stop lights? What are some common myths about car dealerships? Join Scott and Ben as they take a closer look at all things automotive in CarStuff, a podcast by HowStuffWorks. com.

You May Also Like:
CarCast, The Smoking Tire, HowStuffWorks NOW, Under The Hood Automotive Talk Show, Everyday Driver.

The Down & Dirty Radio Show
Host: Jim Beaver
Frequency: Weekly
Average Show Length: 90 Minutes

Description:
Jim Beaver brings you the #1 Action Motorsports Radio Show on the planet covering the world of racing with some of the biggest interviews in motorsports!

You May Also Like:
Stand Up Speak Up, Rotated Views, Jim Beaver's Project Action, Thaddeus Ellenburg's Casual Friday, Sips, Suds, & Smokes

Kinda Funny Games Daily
Hosts: Tim Gettys, Greg Miller, and Colin Moriarty
Frequency: Daily
Average Show Length: 60 Minutes

Description:
Every week Tim Gettys, Greg Miller, and Colin Moriarty talk about everything going on in the video game world. Sometimes there are guests, sometimes there is a wiener dog, all the times Tim will say something ridiculous.

You May Also Like:
PS I Love You XOXO, Kinda Funny Morning Show, The GameOverGreggy Show, Kinda Funny Gamescast, What's Good Games: A Video Game Podcast

Podcast Unlocked
Host: Various
Frequency: Weekly
Average Show Length: 60 Minutes

Description:
Love video games? IGN's Podcast Unlocked is your source for everything Xbox One. If you live and breathe Halo, Gears of War, Forza, and more, Podcast Unlocked has you covered. Tune in every

week for the latest video game news for Xbox One and Xbox Live junkies around the globe.

You May Also Like:
PS I Love You XOXO, Kinda Funny Gamescast, The GameOverGreggy Show, The Game Informer Show, Major Nelson Radio

Nintendo Voice Chat
Host: Various
Frequency: Weekly
Average Show Length: 60 Minutes

Description:
IGN editors discuss all things Nintendo. Now you're playing with power!

You May Also Like:
PS I Love You XOXO, Kinda Funny Gamescast, The GameOverGreggy Show, Kinda Funny Games Daily, The Game Informer Show.

The Giant Beastcast
Host: Giant Bomb
Frequency: Weekly
Average Show Length: 120 Minutes

Description:
The Giant Bomb East team gathers to talk about the week in video games, their lives, and basically anything that interests them. All from New York City!

You May Also Like:
Giant Bombcast, Kinda Funny Gamescast, Waypoint Radio, Idle Thumbs, 8-4 Play.

Glitch Please
Hosts: Gus, Ashley, Ryan
Frequency: Weekly
Average Show Length: 60 Minutes

Description:
Have you ever played a video game and thought, "Hey, games are pretty cool. Except when they're all broken and glitchy. I wish I knew if other people felt the same way." It's a desolate world out there, but GREAT NEWS! You're not alone after all. Join Gus, Ashley, Ryan, and friends from the Rooster Teeth crew to discuss the latest games, talk through issues that impact the gaming industry, digest the latest news, respond to your carefully crafted emails, search for more synonyms to make "talk" sound exciting, and occasionally pretend to be professional about the whole thing (and fail with style).

You May Also Like:
Filmhaus Podcast, Kinda Funny Morning Show, Kinda Funny Games Daily, Internet Box, The Coe Show

The Instance: The Podcast for Lovers of Blizzard Games
Host: Scott Johnson
Frequency: Weekly
Average Show Length: 60 Minutes

Description:
The Instance: Weekly radio for fans and lovers of World of Warcraft. We don't take sides, we don't whine, we just give you the facts, news and tips that you want and need for your favorite online addiction. Come meet us at the stone for another Instance!

You May Also Like:
Convert to Raid Presents: The podcast for World of Warcraft and other Blizzard Games!, The Angry Chicken: A Hearthstone Podcast, All Things Azeroth - Your World of Warcraft Podcast, World of Warcast: A World of Warcraft Podcast, Overwatchers: The Overwatch Podcast.

The G Club
Host: Game Grumps
Frequency: Weekly
Average Show Length: 90 Minutes

Description:
The G Club is Game Grumps' news, media, and pop culture podcast thing! Fill your earholes with loud arguments from everyone around the Game Grumps office!

You May Also Like:
Before the Grumps, SuperMegaCast, Dragons In Places, SleepyCabin, Schmucks Podcast.

The Broman Podcast
Host: Ben Broman
Frequency: Daily
Average Show Length: 60 Minutes

Description:
The official podcast of Ben "ProfessorBroman" Bowman. Listen now or tune in three times a week to get insight and answers live.

You May Also Like:
The Jam, Gaming 101, The Worst Radio Show, Rageless Roundtable

The GameOverGreggy Show
Hosts: Greg Miller, Colin Moriarty, Tim Gettys, Nick Scarpino
Frequency: Weekly
Average Show Length: 90 Minutes

Description:
New Episode Every Friday Watch The Video Version! youtube.com/ kindafunny Every week Greg Miller, Tim Gettys, and Nick Scarpino each bring a random topic they hope will make you laugh. If they fail, at least there's a wiener dog to look at.

You May Also Like:
Podcast Beyond, Kinda Funny Games Daily

Kinda Funny Gamescast
Hosts: Tim Gettys, Greg Miller, Colin Moriarty
Frequency: Weekly
Average Show Length: 60 Minutes

Description:
New Episode Every Friday Watch The Video Version! youtube.com/ kindafunnygames Every week Tim Gettys and Greg Miller talk about everything going on in the video game world. Sometimes there are guests, sometimes there is a wiener dog, all the times Tim will say something ridiculous.

You May Also Like:
Podcast Beyond, Game Scoop!, Podcast Unlocked, Kinda Funny Games Daily, Kinda Funny Morning Show

Super Best Friendcast!
Host: Various
Frequency: Weekly
Average Show Length: 180 Minutes

Description:
Every week, the creators of Super Best Friends Play discuss the best and worst of the videogame industry, pop culture and get excessively hyped about things for no reason.

You May Also Like:
SleepyCabin, The Co-optional Podcast, Giant Bombcast, The Giant Beastcast, Jimquisition

Waypoint Radio
Hosts: Austin Walker, Patrick Klepek
Frequency: Daily
Average Show Length: 90 Minutes

Description:
What's good, Internet? Join Waypoint's Austin Walker and Patrick Klepek twice a week, as they break down the biggest stories in

video games and unfairly compare everything to Dark Souls.

You May Also Like:
Giant Bomb Presents, The Giant Beastcast, Friends at the Table, Idle Thumbs, Idle Thumbs

What's Good Games: A Video Game Podcast
Hosts: Andrea Rene, Alexa Ray Corriea, Brittney Brombacher, Kristine Steimer
Frequency: Weekly
Average Show Length: 120 Minutes

Description:
A weekly video game podcast for the nerd-inclined! Join Andrea Rene, Alexa Ray Corriea, Brittney Brombacher, and Kristine Steimer as they analyze the week's video game news, give hands-on impressions of upcoming titles, discuss your questions, and have a little bit of "off topic" conversation. Also, what's a gaming podcast without some alcohol from time to time?

You May Also Like:
Pockets Full of Soup, The Lobby, Kinda Funny Games Daily, Kinda Funny Morning Show, Colin's Last Stand: Fireside Chats

CoolGames Inc
Hosts: Griffin McElroy, Nick Robinson
Frequency: Weekly
Average Show Length: 60 Minutes

Description:
Join Griffin McElroy and Nick Robinson as they create a new video game every week – with your help.

You May Also Like:
Wonderful!, The McElroy Brothers Will Be In Trolls 2, Til Death Do Us Blart, My Brother, My Brother And Me

GOVERNMENT & ORGANIZATIONS

2018 Gov & Org Top Pick
Radiolab Presents: More Perfect
Host: Jad Abumrad
Frequency: Weekly
Average Show Length: 60 Minutes

Radiolab's More Perfect is a series about the Supreme Court. More Perfect explores how cases deliberated inside the rarefied world of the Supreme Court affect our lives far away from the bench. Produced by WNYC Studios, home of other great podcasts such as Death, Sex & Money, Freakonomics Radio, On the Media, and Here's the Thing.

You May Also Like:
Embedded, Invisibilia, Reply All

The Uncertain Hour – Marketplace
Host: Krissy Clark
Frequency: Monthly
Average Show Length: 30 Minutes

Description:
In The Uncertain Hour, host Krissy Clark dives into one controversial topic each season to reveal the surprising origin stories of our economy. From the Marketplace Wealth & Poverty Desk, each season goes beyond buzzwords to bust longstanding myths and uncover surprising backstories. Because the things we fight the most about are the things we know the least about.

You May Also Like:
The Impact, The United States of Anxiety, There Goes the Neighborhood

What Trump Can Teach Us About Con Law
Host: Roman Mars
Frequency: Monthly
Average Show Length: 30 Minutes

Description:
This show is a weekly, fun, casual Con Law 101 class that uses the tumultuous and erratic activities of the executive branch under Trump to teach us all about the US Constitution.

You May Also Like:
Every Little Thing, Undone, Uncivil

Zero Blog Thirty
Host: Chaps McNealy
Frequency: Monthly
Average Show Length: 60 Minutes

Description:
From bombs, bullets, and bad guys to politics, pop culture and all things problematic: Zero Blog Thirty is the stories you might know told from a slightly different perspective that was forged through

war, wit, and wounds.

You May Also Like:
Young & Happy, Barstool Rundown, The Dave Portnoy Show

First Mondays
Hosts: Ian Samuel, Dan Epps
Frequency: Daily
Average Show Length: 90 Minutes

Description:
First Mondays is an entertaining podcast about the Supreme Court, co-hosted by Ian Samuel and Dan Epps.

You May Also Like:
U.S. Supreme Court Oral Arguments, Oral Argument, Slate's Amicus With Dahlia Lithwick

FieldCraft Survival
Host: Mike Glover
Frequency: weekly
Average Show Length: 60 Minutes

Description:
Welcome to the FieldCraft Survival Podcast, an informative series in survival, tactics, defense, politics, guns, fitness, off-roading, military, and gear.

You May Also Like:
Global Recon, Mentors for Military Podcast, SOFREP Radio

U.S. Supreme Court Oral Arguments
Host: Various
Frequency: Daily
Average Show Length: 60 Minutes

Description:
Oral arguments before the Supreme Court of the United States.

SOFREP Radio
Hosts: Jack Murphy, Jason Delgado
Frequency: Weekly
Average Show Length: 120 Minutes

Description:
Special operations military news and straight talk with the guys.
Hosted by Army Ranger/Green Beret Jack Murphy, Marine Scout
Sniper Jason Delgado, and New York Festivals award winning
radio producer Ian Scotto. As seen ranked #1 in Apple Podcasts
government category.

You May Also Like:
Global Recon, Team Never Quit Podcast, Inside The Team Room

Global Recon
Host: Chantel Taylor
Frequency: Weekly
Average Show Length: 90 Minutes

Description:
Welcome to the Global Recon Podcast! Hosted by John Hendricks a
civilian and the owner of Global Recon co-hosted by Chantel Taylor
a former British Army Combat Medic and the first British woman
in history to kill an enemy in combat. We discuss world events, sit
down with special operators from across the globe, touch on tactical
medicine, mindset, politics, and history.

You May Also Like:
SOFREP Radio, FieldCraft Survival, The Sheepdog Project

A Sustainable Mind
Host: Marjorie Alexander
Frequency: Weekly
Average Show Length: 30 Minutes

Description:
A Sustainable Mind is a podcast created for you, the ecopreneur,
environmental activist, sustainability enthusiast, grassroots organizer,

or those curious about eco-friendly lifestyles. If you are looking to get inspired, motivated and take ACTION to be the change you want to see in the world you are in the right place.

You May Also Like:
Sustainable World Radio, Infinite Earth Radio, The Sustainable Living Podcast

The Bernie Sanders Show
Host: Senator Bernie Sanders
Frequency: Weekly
Average Show Length: 20 Minutes

Description:
Sen. Bernie Sanders, along with leading activists, journalists, policymakers, artists, visionaries and revolutionaries, talk about the resistance, the political revolution and moving forward on a progressive agenda.

You May Also Like:
Pod Save the People, The Bernie Sanders Show, Intercepted with Jeremy Scahill

Scholars Strategy Network's No Jargon
Host: Avi Green
Frequency: Weekly
Average Show Length: 30 Minutes

Description:
No Jargon, the Scholars Strategy Network's weekly podcast, presents interviews with top university scholars on the politics, policy problems, and social issues facing the nation. Powerful research, intriguing perspectives -- and no jargon.

You May Also Like:
I Think You're Interesting, Worldly, The Impact

The CSIS Podcast
Host: Colm Quinn
Frequency: Weekly
Average Show Length: 20 Minutes

Description:
Each episode dissects the big (and soon-to-be big) stories of the week in U.S. foreign policy and international affairs. Hosted by Colm Quinn.

You May Also Like:
CFR On the Record, The World Next Week, Foreign Affairs Unedited

The PayLess Murders
Host: John Christgau
Frequency: Weekly
Average Show Length: 30 Minutes

Description:
This podcast is the story of The PayLess Murders, California's longest old cold triple homicide, told in the voices & words of those who lived the story.

You May Also Like:
Leap in the Dark: a podcast, 12-26-75, The Grave Truth Podcast

Intersections
Host: Adrianna Pita
Frequency: Weekly
Average Show Length: 60 Minutes

Description:
Economic recovery. Elections. Terrorism. Global poverty. Trade. Tune in to Intersections, a podcast from the Brookings Institution, where two experts delve into the varying angles of the complicated issues facing our nation and the world.

You May Also Like:
Events from the Brookings Institution, 5 on 45

Faithfactor Impact
Host: Jessie Everline
Frequency: Weekly
Average Show Length: 60 Minutes

Description:
On FaithFactor Impact, Jessie Everline interviews today's top thought leaders in the nonprofit and social sector. From the nonprofit community leader to the social intreprenuer, this is where you get timely inspiration, valuable content, ideas you can implement and connections that will keep you going. Each podcast episode features a successful thought leader who shares their story, some best practices, and their approach for cultivating strategic partnerships.

You May Also Like:
Your Blessed Life, Tony Martignetti Nonprofit Radio, Social Good Instigators Podcast

Armed American Radio
Host: Various
Frequency: Weekly
Average Show Length: 60 Minutes

Description:
Armed American Radio (AAR) is the official radio program of The United States Concealed Carry Association.

You May Also Like:
Student of the Gun Radio, NRA News, Bullets with AWR Hawkins

2017 California Driver Audio Handbook
Host: Various
Frequency: Seasonal
Average Show Length: 30 Minutes

Description:
Listen to the free version of the 2017 California Driver Handbook to help you study for the written driver license exam.

PolicyCast
Host: Matt Cadwallader
Frequency: Weekly
Average Show Length: 30 Minutes

Description:
Public policy affects every aspect of modern life, but while political skirmishes routinely dominate the headlines, the details of how practitioners in all walks of public life can pursue good governance and and principled leadership too often get lost.

You May Also Like:
The Brookings Cafeteria, Intersections, CFR On the Record

Veteran Podcast And Military News Talk Radio Including Special Operations And Military Technology
Host: Various
Frequency: Weekly
Average Show Length: 120 Minutes

Description:
Teaching strategies, classroom management, education reform, educational technology -- if it has something to do with teaching, we're talking about it. Jennifer Gonzalez interviews educators, students, administrators and parents about the psychological and social dynamics of school, trade secrets, and other juicy things you'll never learn in a textbook.

You May Also Like:
Inside The Team Room, SOFREP Radio, Global Recon

Sasquatch Syndicate
Host: Chuck & Paul
Frequency: Weekly
Average Show Length: 60 Minutes

Description:
Join Sasquatch Syndicate for expert opinion, eye-witness accounts, and special guests. Sasquatch Syndicate is a Washington State Non-

profit organization whose mission is to promote the research, and discovery of Sasquatch.

You May Also Like:
Monster X Radio, SasWhat: A Podcast about Bigfoot, The Confessionals

Jay Sekulow Live Radio Show
Host: Jay Sekulow
Frequency: Daily
Average Show Length: 60 Minutes

Description:
Listen to our daily radio program, Jay Sekulow Live! for issues that matter most to you - national security, protecting America's families, and protecting human life. The reports are brought to you by the American Center for Law & Justice (ACLJ), a nonprofit organization specializing constitutional law and based in Washington, D.C.

You May Also Like:
WallBuilders Live! with David Barton & Rick Green, Understanding the Times on OnePlace.com, The Laura Ingraham Show Podcast

CFR On the Record
Host: Various
Frequency: Weekly
Average Show Length: 60 Minutes

Description:
A chance to go inside Council on Foreign Relations events. Listen to world leaders and foreign policy experts discuss and debate the most pressing issues in international affairs.

You May Also Like:
The CSIS Podcast, Foreign Affairs Unedited, Carnegie Council Audio Podcast

HEALTH

2018 Health Top Pick
The School of Greatness
Host: Lewis Howes
Frequency: Weekly
Average Show Length: 60 Minutes

Lewis Howes is a NYT bestselling author, lifestyle entrepreneur, former pro athlete and world record holder in football. The goal of the School of Greatness is to share inspiring stories from the most brilliant business minds, world class athletes and influential celebrities on the planet; to help you find out what makes great people great.

You May Also Like:
The Tony Robbins Podcast, The GaryVee Audio Experience, The Art of Charm

The Psych Central Show: Candid Chat on Mental Health & Psychology
Hosts: Gabe Howard, Vincent M. Wales
Frequency: Weekly
Average Show Length: 30 Minutes

Description:
The Psych Central Show is a weekly podcast that offers a candid, interesting, and in-depth look into all things mental health and psychology.

You May Also Like:
Thaddeus Ellenburg's Casual Friday, Jim Beaver's Project Action, Stand Up Speak Up

The Art of Charm
Host: Jordan Harbinger
Frequency: Daily
Average Show Length: 60 Minutes

Description:
Social science, behavioral economics, cognitive psychology -- sound complex? Let's fix that. The Art of Charm Podcast is where self-motivated guys and gals, just like you, come to learn from a diverse mix of experienced mentors, including the world's best professional and academic minds, scientists, innovators, coaches, relationship experts, entrepreneurs, bestselling authors, and other brilliant minds.

You May Also Like:
The Art of Manliness, The School of Greatness with Lewis Howes, The Tim Ferriss Show

Kwik Brain: Memory Improvement
Host: Jim Kwik
Frequency: weekly
Average Show Length: 15 Minutes

Description:
Kwik Brain is a fun, fast-paced show designed to help busy people

learn and achieve anything in a fraction of the time! Your coach, Jim Kwik (his real name), is the brain & memory trainer to elite mental performers, including many of the world's leading CEO's and celebrities. In this easy to digest bite-sized podcast, you will discover Kwik's favorite shortcuts to read faster, remember more, and 'supercharge' your greatest wealth-building asset: your brain.

You May Also Like:
Impact Theory with Tom Bilyeu, The Model Health Show, The James Altucher Show

Success Sculpting Show with Stephen Pierce
Host: Stephen Pierce
Frequency: Weekly
Average Show Length: 60 Minutes

Description:
The Success Sculpting Show podcast with Stephen Pierce, brings you the right information right now to sculpt a more meaningful and memorable life of success. Join us each week to discover success gems to help you grow your mental toughness, expand your will to win and multiply your results.

You May Also Like:
Life With Champons, Breaking The Underdog Curse, Are You Hearing This!

Crossroads of Health
Host: Rick Simpson
Frequency: Monthly
Average Show Length: 60 Minutes

Description:
Crossroads of Health focuses on a wide variety of topics including Heart Health, Joint Health, Adrenal Health, Thyroid function, Men & Women's Health, and so much more.

You May Also Like:
Dr. Lars Dingman, Female Mixing Engineers Music Podcast

Breaking The Underdog Curse
Host: Dr. Don MacDonald
Frequency: Weekly
Average Show Length: 45 Minutes

Description:
Breaking "The Underdog Curse" is a show for vitalistic Chiropractors about breaking free from limiting beliefs, and how to overcome being stuck as an underdog. Your Host Dr. Don MacDonald is a Chiropractor, coach and the author of the bestselling book "The Underdog Curse". Hear Dr. Don's personal interviews with thought leaders, bestselling authors, and Chiropractors from around the world. All designed to inspire you, challenge you and help you live more aligned with who you truly are.

You May Also Like:
Pick the Brain Podcast, Life With Chapmans, Laser Sandwich

Coaching for Geeks
Hosts: Robin Bates, Austin Toloza, Rami the Gutsy Geek
Frequency: Weekly
Average Show Length: 60 Minutes

Description:
The geek shall inherit the earth, but some of us need a little bit of help gaining the XP to get there. Your award-winning, international geek experts, Coach Robin Bates, Rami the Gutsy Geek, and Coach Austin Toloza, cover confidence, dating, self-belief, fitness, style, careers, relationships, planning for success and everything you need to live the best geeky life. Geek guests from the worlds of gaming, cosplay, comics, psychology, YouTube, and much more share their experiences and challenges of getting ahead. With live plays of tabletop RPGs, attendance at cons, shows and more, our team of coaches will change your life, and do their best to not be wanky about it. Hit Start to Begin - it's Coaching for Geeks!

You May Also Like:
Beyond the States: College in Europe, Crossroads of Health, Weird Frakin' Shtako

Optimal Living Daily
Host: Justin Malik
Frequency: Daily
Average Show Length: 10 Minutes

Description:
I read you the best content on personal development, minimalism, productivity, and more, with author permission.

You May Also Like:
The Minimalists Podcast, Good Life Project, The Daily Boost

The Minimalists Podcast
Hosts: Joshua Fields Millburn, Ryan Nicodemus
Frequency: Weekly
Average Show Length: 120 Minutes

Description:
Joshua Fields Millburn & Ryan Nicodemus discuss living a meaningful life with less.

You May Also Like:
Happier with Gretchen Rubin, Optimal Living Daily, Good Life Project

The Rich Roll Podcast
Host: Rich Roll
Frequency: Weekly
Average Show Length: 30 Minutes

Description:
A master-class in personal and professional development, ultra-athlete, wellness evangelist and bestselling author Rich Roll delves deep with the world's brightest and most thought provoking thought leaders to educate, inspire and empower you to unleash your best, most authentic self.

You May Also Like:
No Meat Athlete Radio, Ben Greenfield Fitness, Bulletproof Radio

The Toxic People Detox
Host: Dr. Shayla D. Williams
Frequency: Weekly
Average Show Length: 20 Minutes

Description:
Fighting the toxic people in your life isn't worth the serious health threats that come with the territory. Diabetes. High blood pressure. Excessive weight gain. Bankruptcy. And repeated broken hearts. Yes, you have a right to be angry at the injustice caused by the toxic people in your life. But you also have a right -- an obligation -- to fight towards making your situation better.

You May Also Like:
The Apathetic Vegan, A Well Run Life, Beyond the States: College in Europe

Good Life Project
Host: Jonathan Fields
Frequency: Weekly
Average Show Length: 60 Minutes

Description:
Inspirational, intimate and disarmingly-unfiltered conversations about living a fully-engaged, fiercely-connected and meaning-drenched life. From iconic world-shakers like Elizabeth Gilbert, Brene Brown, Sir Ken Robinson, Seth Godin and Gretchen Rubin to everyday guests, every story matters.

You May Also Like:
Happier with Gretchen Rubin, Optimal Living Daily, The Minimalists

Bulletproof Radio
Host: Dave Asprey
Frequency: Weekly
Average Show Length: 60 Minutes

Description:
Welcome to being Bulletproof, the State of High Performance where

you take control and improve your biochemistry, your body, and your mind so they work in unison, helping you execute at levels far beyond what you'd expect, without burning out, getting sick, or just acting like a stressed-out a-hole. It used to take a lifetime to radically rewire the human body and mind this way. Technology has changed the rules. Follow along as Dave Asprey and guests provide you with everything you need to upgrade your mind, body, and life.

You May Also Like:
The Fat-Burning Man Show, Ben Greenfield Fitness, Robb Wolf

Finding Mastery: Conversations with Michael Gervais
Host: Michael Gervais
Frequency: Weekly
Average Show Length: 60 Minutes

Description:
In the trenches with some of the best performers in the world — some who shift how we conceive what's possible — others who have pushed their own boundaries — ranging from hall of fame athletes to action sport game-changers, entrepreneurs, Mixed Martial Artists, to musicians who influence the rhythm of the world.

You May Also Like:
Minutes on Mastery, The Rich Roll Podcast, Outside Podcast

Savage Lovecast
Host: Dan Savage
Frequency: Weekly
Average Show Length: 50 Minutes

Description:
Dan Savage, America's only advice columnist, answers your sex questions and yaps about politics.

You May Also Like:
Death, Sex & Money, Dear Sugars, Modern Love

The Virtual Couch
Host: Anthony Overbay
Frequency: Seasonal
Average Show Length: 90 Minutes

Description:
A marriage and family therapist, humor columnist and motivational speaker who works with a large number of individuals and couples in a variety of areas including marriage, sexual addiction, and parenting. Tony, and his guests, hope to provide listeners with tools and strategies to help break negative patterns and embrace new and exciting challenges in their lives.

You May Also Like:
Brown Chicken Brown Cow Podcast, Bringing Grace to the Nations, Healthy Made Easy

Business and Biceps
Hosts: Cory Gregory, John Fosco
Frequency: Weekly
Average Show Length: 60 Minutes

Description:
Focusing on a wide range of topics, including business, sports, pop culture, what's trending, fitness, fighting and motivation, Cory and John rely on their successful backgrounds to give unique thoughts and outside-the-box insights that are sure to make you stronger in business and in the gym.

You May Also Like:
The Young and Hungry Firecast, The Barbell Life, Westside Barbell

The Keto Diet Podcast
Host: Leanne Vogel
Frequency: Weekly
Average Show Length: 60 Minutes

Description:
Support your low-carb, high-fat life with The Keto Diet Podcast, a

fresh take on ketogenic living with Holistic Nutritionist and keto enthusiast, Leanne Vogel of HealthfulPursuit.com. Interviews with thought leaders, keto veterans, and exclusive content delivering powerful actions to understanding keto, developing a ketogenic diet that works for you, overcoming daily keto struggles, boosting body confidence, shedding weight, and more.

You May Also Like:
Keto Talk With Jimmy Moore & Dr. Will Cole, Keto For Women Show, The Livin' La Vida Low-Carb Show With Jimmy Moore

10% Happier with Dan Harris
Host: Dan Harris
Frequency: Weekly
Average Show Length: 60 Minutes

Description:
Can you be an ambitious person and still strive for enlightenment (whatever that means)? New episodes every Wednesday morning.

You May Also Like:
Happier with Gretchen Rubin, The Minimalists Podcast, Good Life Project

The Brendan Show
Host: Brendon Burchard
Frequency: Weekly
Average Show Length: 60 Minutes

Description:
Every week, Brendon shares what he's struggling with, working on and marching towards - and how we can all live an extraordinary life. This is an intimate and inspiring look into the life and strategies of one of the most watched, followed and quoted personal development trainers in history.

You May Also Like:
The School of Greatness with Lewis Howes, Build Your Tribe, The Chalene Show

Therapy for Black Girls
Host: Joy Harden Bradford
Frequency: Weekly
Average Show Length: 50 Minutes

Description:
The Therapy for Black Girls Podcast is a weekly chat about all things mental health, personal development, and all the small decisions we can make to become the best possible versions of ourselves. Join your host, Dr. Joy Harden Bradford, a licensed Psychologist in Atlanta, Georgia, as she offers practical tips and strategies to improve your mental health, discusses the latest news and trends in mental health, pulls back the curtain on what happens in therapy sessions, and answers your listener questions.

You May Also Like:
Black Girl In Om, Black Girl Podcast, Black Girl Boss Podcast

The Daily Boost: Best Daily Motivation
Host: Scott Smith
Frequency: Weekly
Average Show Length: 15 Minutes

Description:
Need Motivation? The best daily motivation is The Daily Boost! Find out what makes you happy! Reduce your stress! Get inspired! Master life skills like lifestyle design, balance, communication, career advancement and enjoy more success. The Daily Boost is the world's most popular daily motivation program. Scott Smith delivers a unique, straight talking, real, very funny, and extreamly effective strategies that will give you amazing results! The Daily Boost has been iTunes top ranked self-help program since 2004 – give it a listen and find out why so many people around the world make The Daily Boost part their day... every day.

You May Also Like:
Optimal Living Daily, Good Life Project, Operation Self Reset

Ben Greenfield Fitness: Diet, Fat Loss and Performance
Host: Ben Greenfield
Frequency: Weekly
Average Show Length: 60 Minutes

Description:
Free fitness, nutrition, biohacking, fat loss, anti-aging and cutting-edge health advice from BenGreenfieldFitness.com! Tune in to the latest research, interviews with exercise, diet and medical professionals, and an entertaining mash-up of ancestral wisdom and modern science, along with Q&A's and mind-body-spirit optimizing content from America's top personal trainer.

You May Also Like:
Bulletproof Radio, The Fat-Burning Man Show by Abel James: The Future of Health & Performance, Mind Pump: Raw Fitness Truth

Mark Bell's PowerCast
Host: Mark Bell
Frequency: Weekly
Average Show Length: 90 Minutes

Description:
Mark Bell's PowerCast is a weekly show featuring humorous and informative conversations with top names in powerlifting, bodybuilding, strongman, athletic training, coaching, CrossFit, and entrepreneurship. It is hosted by pro powerlifter, inventor of the Sling Shot, and magazine publisher Mark Bell, along with co-host Jim McDonald. Mark was featured in the 2008 Sundance documentary "Bigger Stronger Faster" and the 2015 Tribeca documentary "Prescription Thugs" and Jim was one of the first consistent creators of powerlifting content in the early days of YouTube.

You May Also Like:
The JuggLife, Barbell Shrugged - Talking Training w/ CrossFit Games Athletes, Strength Coaches & More, Physique Science Radio

Pick the Brain Podcast
Hosts: Erin Falconer, Jeremy Fisher
Frequency: Weekly
Average Show Length: 30 Minutes

Description:
From the Self-Improvement Phenomenon blog PickTheBrain.com comes the Pick the Brain Podcast, the show where we pick the brains of the brightest minds in productivity, health, and self improvement.

You May Also Like:
Breaking The Underdog Curse, Laser Sandwich, Just Ask David

The Secret To Success
Host: Eric Thomas
Frequency: Weekly
Average Show Length: 90 Minutes

Description:
From homeless, high school drop out to Entrepreneur, C.E.O. and Ph.D.! Hear first hand how Eric was able to defy the odds, and single-handedly break the negative generational cycles that plagued his family for decades. Join the conversation with ET and co-host Carlas Quinney Jr. and learn how you too can create the life you deserve.

You May Also Like:
Cardone Zone, The MFCEO Project, The Model Health Show

Onnit Podcast
Host: Kyle Kingsbury
Frequency: Weekly
Average Show Length: 60 Minutes

Description:
Achieve peak performance in everyday life. Learn mindset, diet, supplement and fitness regimens from the brightest minds and strongest athletes in the world.

KIDS & FAMILY

2018 Kids & Family Top Pick
Dream Big Podcast
Hosts: Eva Karpman, Olga Karpman
Frequency: Weekly
Average Show Length: 30 Minutes

The Dream Big Podcast is a family-friendly podcast inspiring kids (and adults!) to pursue their passions in life and take action to make their dreams a reality. Your hosts Eva Karpman (currently 7-years-old in 2nd grade) and mom Olga Karpman interview world-class performers who do what they love and live their dreams each and every day.

You May Also Like:
Sips, Suds, & Smokes, Thaddeus Ellenburg's Casual Friday, Jim Beaver's Project Action

Reading With Your Kids Podcast
Host: Kitty Felde
Frequency: Daily
Average Show Length: 45 Minutes

Description:
Reading With Your Kids is all about encouraging parents to read with their kids, and cook with their kids, and do activities with their kids, and experience tv, movies and music together. In other words, our podcast is all about helping parents build stronger relationships with their kids.

You May Also Like:
Dad As Hell, NuChannel Sports Podcast, Edyne Plancy Show

Story Pirates
Host: Various
Frequency: Weekly
Average Show Length: 20 Minutes

Description:
Story Pirates is a group of world-class actors, comedians, improvisers and musicians who adapt stories written by kids into sketch comedy and musical theater.

You May Also Like:
Tumble Science Podcast for Kids, The Alien Adventures of Finn Caspian: Science Fiction for Kids, Short and Curly

Wow in the World
Hosts: Guy Raz, Mindy Thomas
Frequency: Weekly
Average Show Length: 30 Minutes

Description:
Wow in the World is a podcast and a new way for families to connect, look up and discover the wonders in the world around them. Every episode, hosts Mindy and Guy guide curious kids and their grown-ups away from their screens and on a journey. Through

a combination of careful scientific research and fun, we'll go inside our brains, out into space, and deep into the coolest new stories in science and technology.

You May Also Like:
Brains On! Science podcast for kids, Tumble Science Podcast for Kids, Stories Podcast - A Free Children's Story Podcast for Bedtime, Car Rides, and Kids of All Ages!

Pickle
Hosts: Carl Smith, Shumita Basu
Frequency: Seasonal
Average Show Length: 30 Minutes

Description:
Is it ever okay to tell a lie? What makes a real friend? And here's a question: How much is a person's life worth? Yikes, that's a tough one! Join the cast of Pickle as we explore life's stickiest wickets, with the help of curious kids --and the occasional elephant. It's philosophy, made fun.

You May Also Like:
Radiolab, Freakonomics Radio, Radiolab Presents: More Perfect

This Podcast Has Fleas
Host: Various
Frequency: Daily
Average Show Length: 25 Minutes

Description:
What happens when rival pets have dueling podcasts? Find out as Jones (Jay Pharoah), a slick cat with a taste for auto tune, faces off with Waffles (Emily Lynne), a dog who can't help chewing her microphone. Also starring Benny the gerbil (Eugene Mirman) and Mr. Glub the goldfish (Alec Baldwin).

You May Also Like:
Pinna, The Past and The Curious, The Kid Stuff Podcast

The Longest Shortest Time
Host: Hillary Frank
Frequency: Weekly
Average Show Length: 60 Minutes

Description:
The parenting show for for everyone. Hosted by This American Life contributor and author Hillary Frank.

You May Also Like:
Respectful Parenting: Janet Lansbury Unruffled, One Bad Mother, Slate's Mom and Dad Are Fighting

Confessions of a Terrible Husband
Host: Nick Pavlidis
Frequency: Monthly
Average Show Length: 60 Minutes

Description:
Confessions of a Terrible Husband is a marriage podcast for people who are looking for real advice from the trenches and who are committed to taking personal responsibility over improving their relationships.

You May Also Like:
The Stupendous Marriage Show, First Year Marriage Show, Smalley Marriage Radio

Five Minutes With Dad
Hosts: Pavlos, Angela, Nick Pavlidis
Frequency: Weekly
Average Show Length: 10 Minutes

Description:
Five Minutes With Dad stars toddlers Pavlos and Angela Pavlidis and their thirty-something dad Nick Pavlidis. This is the podcast where you get to listen in on a little father-son and daddy-daughter time and learn about great resources to connect with your kids. If you're looking for family, parenting, or kids activities - or if you're looking for

motivation and ideas on how to spend a little more quality time with your children, you came to the right place!

You May Also Like:
Little Stories for Tiny People: Anytime and bedtime stories for kids, What If World - Stories for Kids, Ear Snacks

Brains On! Science Podcast For Kids
Host: Molly Bloom
Frequency: Weekly
Average Show Length: 30 Minutes

Description:
Brains On!® is a science podcast for curious kids and adults from American Public Media. Co-hosted each week by kid scientists and reporters from public radio, we ask questions ranging from the science behind sneezing to how to translate the purr of cats, and go wherever the answers take us.

You May Also Like:
Tumble Science Podcast for Kids, Wow in the World, Stories Podcast

Dads With Swag
Host: Sean Alfonso
Frequency: Weekly
Average Show Length: 60 Minutes

Description:
Motivational Life Coach Sean Alfonso has been a successful entrepreneur and businessman for over 25 years. All of this while juggling being a divorced parent of two amazing young girls. Sean has found the way to balance professional success while achieving meaningful personal relationships.

You May Also Like:
The Minimalists Podcast, Good Life Project, The Daily Boost

Focus on the Family Broadcast
Hosts: Jim Daly, John Fuller
Frequency: Daily
Average Show Length: 60 Minutes

Description:
Focus on the Family is a half-hour daily dose of encouragement and advice for the family with Jim Daly and John Fuller. Focus on the Family began airing in 1977. It is now carried daily on 2,000 radio outlets in the United States and has become one of today's most recognized Christian radio programs.

You May Also Like:
FamilyLife Today® with Dennis Rainey, Family Talk on OnePlace.com, God Centered Mom Podcast

Stories Podcast
Host: Amanda Weldin
Frequency: Weekly
Average Show Length: 20 Minutes

Description:
On the Stories Podcast, we perform a new story for your children every week. The stories range from retellings of fairy tales like Snow White to classic stories like Peter Rabbit and even completely original works. Everything is G rated and safe for all ages.

You May Also Like:
Storynory - Stories for Kids, Brains On! Science podcast for kids, Tumble Science Podcast for Kids

Storynory - Stories for Kids
Host: Natasha
Frequency: Weekly
Average Show Length: 15 Minutes

Description:
Storynory brings you an audio story every week. Each one is beautifully read by Natasha and friends. Let Natasha's voice beguile

you with classic fairy tales, new children's stories, poems, myths, adventures and romance.

You May Also Like:
Stories Podcast, Car Rides, and Kids of All Ages!, Brains On!, Story Time

Respectful Parenting: Janet Lansbury Unruffled
Host: Janet Lansbury
Frequency: Weekly
Average Show Length: 20 Minutes

Description:
Each episode addresses a reader's parenting issue through the lens of Janet's respectful parenting philosophy.

You May Also Like:
The Longest Shortest Time, The Mighty Mommy's Quick and Dirty Tips for Practical Parenting, One Bad Mother

The Fatherly Podcast
Host: Joshua David Stein
Frequency: Weekly
Average Show Length: 30 Minutes

Description:
Welcome to The Fatherly Podcast. Hosted by Joshua David Stein, the Fatherly Podcast is the perfect podcast for imperfect parents. Join us as we talk to documentarians, actors, athletes, writers and more about the joys and challenges of being a dad. There's also a theme song, which is rad; a segment called "Oh, hey science" where we talk about the latest studies and findings; and an interview with a child.

You May Also Like:
The Modern Dads Podcast, Work and Life with Stew Friedman, The Life of Dad Show

God Centered Mom Podcast
Host: Heather MacFadyen
Frequency: Weekly
Average Show Length: 20 Minutes

Description:
In this podcast Heather interviews guests about staying God-centered in a shaky mom world.

You May Also Like:
InspiredToAction, Risen Motherhood, At Home With Sally

For Crying Out Loud
Hosts: Lynette Carolla, Stefanie Wilder-Taylor
Frequency: Weekly
Average Show Length: 60 Minutes

Description:
In this raucous hour of conversations they cover a range of topics from their marriages and kids, to the pros and cons of ferberizing to which one of the Real Housewives have had too much filler (all of them). The format is informative, loose and most of all entertaining.

You May Also Like:
Alison Rosen Is Your New Best Friend, This Life #YOULIVE With Dr Drew, Sword and Scale Rewind

ONE Extraordinary Marriage Show
Hosts: Tony DiLorenzo, Alisa DiLorenzo
Frequency: Weekly
Average Show Length: 30 Minutes

Description:
Is your marriage everything that you want it to be? Are you ready to make a change? Join Tony and Alisa DiLorenzo to create a strong marriage so you can have mind blowing intimacy inside and outside the bedroom. Marriage is not always easy but it's so worth it. Come and make your marriage EXTRAORDINARY!

Focus on the Family Marriage Podcast
Host: John Fuller
Frequency: Weekly
Average Show Length: 10 Minutes

Description:
Timeless wisdom from Focus on the Family that will challenge and encourage you in your marriage.

You May Also Like:
FamilyLife Today, ONE Extraordinary Marriage Show, The Love and Respect Podcast

Focus on the Family Parenting Podcast
Host: John Fuller
Frequency: Weekly
Average Show Length: 10 Minutes

Description:
Need help with raising your kids? Focus on the Family provides tried and true parenting advice to help your children thrive.

You May Also Like:
God Centered Mom Podcast, Parenting On Purpose, The Mighty Mommy's Quick and Dirty Tips for Practical Parenting

Circle Round
Host: Rebecca Sheir
Frequency: Weekly
Average Show Length: 20 Minutes

Description:
Where story time happens all the time.

You May Also Like:
Story Pirates, Eleanor Amplified, Ear Snacks

The Official Adventures in Odyssey Podcast

Hosts: Bob Smithouser, Jesse Florea
Frequency: Weekly
Average Show Length: 30 Minutes

Description:
Created for children ages 8-12 (but loved by listeners of all ages), Adventures in Odyssey is a 30-minute drama that combines the faith lessons parents appreciate with characters and stories that kids love! The official podcast gives behind-the-scenes information on the show, gives deleted scenes and answers fan questions.

You May Also Like:
God Centered Mom Podcast, Read-Aloud Revival, At Home With Sally

Tumble Science Podcast for Kids

Host: Lindsay Patterson
Frequency: Weekly
Average Show Length: 50 Minutes

Description:
Exploring stories of science discovery. Tumble is a science podcast created to be enjoyed by the entire family. Hosted & produced by Lindsay Patterson (science journalist) & Marshall Escamilla (teacher). Visit www.tumblepodcast.com for more information and educational content.

You May Also Like:
Brains On! Science podcast for kids, Stories Podcast, Story Pirates

The Big Boo Cast

Host: Melanie Shankle & Sophie Hudson
Frequency: Weekly
Average Show Length: 60 Minutes

Description:
Authors / speakers Melanie Shankle and Sophie Hudson - also known as Big Mama and BooMama on their blogs - talk about all the

important stuff: faith, family, friends, football, fashion, and food. Plus, of course, their hair.

You May Also Like:
The Popcast With Knox and Jamie, That Sounds Fun with Annie F. Downs, Glorious in the Mundane Podcast with Christy Nockels

At Home With Sally
Host: Sally Clarkson
Frequency: Weekly
Average Show Length: 30 Minutes

Description:
Home is the place where the whispers of God's love are heard regularly, the touch of His hands is given intentionally throughout the day, the words of His encouragement and affirmation pointed to lay the foundation of loving relationships where a woman conducts the beauty of this life within its walls. I hope you will find inspiration to cultivate such a life within the pages of this blog.

You May Also Like:
Read-Aloud Revival, Cultivating the Lovely- The Podcast, Your Morning Basket

Dr. Laura Weekly Podcast
Host: Dr. Laura Schlessinger
Frequency: Once
Average Show Length: 50 Minutes

Description:
As one of the most popular talk show hosts in radio history, Dr. Laura Schlessinger offers no-nonsense advice infused with a strong sense of ethics, accountability, and personal responsibility

You May Also Like:
Uncovered with Dr. Laura Berman: Highlights, The Art of Authenticity, Parenting Great Kids with Dr. Meg Meeker

MUSIC

2018 Music Top Pick
Broken Record
Hosts: Rick Rubin, Malcolm Gladwell
Frequency: Monthly
Average Show Length: 10 Minutes

From Rick Rubin and Malcolm Gladwell, liner notes for the digital age. Digressions, arguments, back-stories, and random things to disagree with about music.

You May Also Like:
Dissect, Whats's Good, Origins, A Waste of Time, Mogul: The Life and Death of Chris Lighty

Turned Up
Hosts: Jake Jones, Robert Venable
Frequency: Weekly
Average Show Length: 60 Minutes

Description:
Producer/audio engineer/professional guitarist, Jake Jones and award winning producer/audio engineer, Robert Venable bring in legendary guests to pull back the curtain and give you a peek into the behind the scenes operation that keeps the music industry running like a well oiled machine. Is that machine starting to break down? Listen and decide for yourself.

You May Also Like:
3 People Like This, Drawing Board Advice Podcast, Why I'm Not... with Brant Pinvidic After Show, Alternative Facts Chicago, Crossroads of Health

Female Mixing Engineers Music Podcast
Host: Darcy Jeavons
Frequency: Weekly
Average Show Length: 60 Minutes

Description:
The Female Mixing Engineers Music Podcast brings to your ears 4 songs created by 4 very talented females in 4 unique home studios. These ladies share their gear, technique, and secrets as to how they have achieved the great sound you have heard. The FME Podcast has been created to help and inspire YOU to make fantastic music in your home studio. Encouraging females to become more involved in the field of audio engineering, as well as entertaining everyone who searches for fabulous original music. You won't just hear this music, you will feel it!

You May Also Like:
3 People Like This, Crossroads of Health, Dr. Lars Dingman - iTunes Psychic, 3 People Like This - The Interviews

The Loudini Rock and Roll Circus
Host: Lou Lombardi
Frequency: Daily
Average Show Length: 45 Minutes

Description:
The Loudini Rock 'n Roll Circus brings you News, Music, Business Tips and Great Rock and Roll by the best emerging Artists.

You May Also Like:
Geekvibes Nation, View From the Penalty Box, DJ Frankie Vazquez - Globalization, Sage Flipping Secrets, GSMC Basketball Podcast

All Songs Considered
Host: Bob Boilen, Rob Hilton
Frequency: Daily
Average Show Length: 40 Minutes

Description:
Hosts/nerds Bob Boilen and Robin Hilton are your friendly music buddies with the week's best new music discoveries, including conversations with emerging artists, icons and more. Hear songs that can completely change your day, with humor, heart and (sometimes) a whole lot of noise.

You May Also Like:
Song Exploder, Snap Judgment, KEXP Song of the Day, The New Yorker Radio Hour, WTF with Marc Maron Podcast

I'll Name This Podcast Later
Host: Joe Budden
Frequency: Weekly
Average Show Length: 60 Minutes

Description:
Joe Budden and his friends Rory & Mal sit down every week to discuss life, music, sex, and more.

Song Exploder
Host: Hrishikesh Hirway
Frequency: Weekly
Average Show Length: 15 Minutes

Description:
Song Exploder is a podcast where musicians take apart their songs, and piece by piece, tell the story of how they were made. Each episode features an artist discussing a song of theirs, breaking down the sounds and ideas that went into the writing and recording.

You May Also Like:
Reply All, All Songs Considered, Surprisingly Awesome, Mystery Show, Heavyweight.

DJ Frankie Vazquez - Globalization
Host: Frankie Vazquez
Frequency: Monthly
Average Show Length: 30 Minutes

Description:
Full Mixes of EDM, House, Mashups, Freestyle, Hip Hop, Reggae, Reggaeton, Top40, Salsa, Bachata.

You May Also Like:
Geekvibes Nation, The Loudini Rock and Roll Circus, Full Court Press | For the Intellectually Curious NBA Fan, Thanks Dad, Lost in America

Drink Champs
Hosts: N.O.R.E, DJ EFN
Frequency: Weekly
Average Show Length: 90 Minutes

Description
Legendary Queens rapper and one half of Capone-n-Noreaga N.O.R.E. alongside Miami hip-hop pioneer DJ EFN come together as the Drink Champs. Listen in as N.O.R.E., DJ EFN and special guests talk over some drinks and discuss everything from current events to old school stories. Nothing is sacred when talking with the Drink

Champs so this show is not for the easily offended!

You May Also Like:
Tax Season, The Joe Budden Podcast, The Combat Jack Show, Rap Radar Podcast, The Brilliant Idiots

The Joe Budden Podcast
Host: Joe Budden
Frequency: Weekly
Average Show Length: 60 Minutes

Description:
Joe Budden and his friends Rory & Mal sit down every week to discuss life, music, sex, and more. Tune in and follow along the crazy adventures of these very random friends.

You May Also Like:
Tax Season, The Combat Jack Show, Drink Champs, The Brilliant Idiots, Rap Radar

Do You Remember? A podcast about Hüsker Dü
Host: Various
Frequency: Daily
Average Show Length: 30 Minutes

Description:
This documentary podcast explores Hüsker Dü's formative years and legacy through rare exclusive interviews with the band, as well as those who were around in the beginning and notable artists who've drawn inspiration from the band. We'll also dive into recordings from Numero Group's new remastered box set of the band's early releases, demos and live recordings.

You May Also Like:
Creative Kontrol, Dogpatch, Rockin' the Suburbs, Culture Creature, The Watt From Pedro Show

Launch Left
Host: Rain Joan
Frequency: Weekly
Average Show Length: 60 Minutes

Description:
Rain Joan of Arc Phoenix and Moon Unit Zappa interview extraordinary minds, mavericks brick throwers, and pioneers in their unique fields. As two women from artistically uncompromising families, Rain and Moon celebrate non-conformists who achieve success by doing it their way, and support 'left of center' emerging artists.

You May Also Like:
I'm Still Here, When to Jump, ZappaCast - The Frank Zappa Podcast, Everything Zappa Podcast

Dissect - A Serialized Music Podcast
Host: Various
Frequency: Weekly
Average Show Length: 30 Minutes

Description:
Dissect is a serialized music podcast that breaks long form music analysis into short, digestible episodes. Each season we pick one album and examine one song per episode, dissecting measure-by-measure, word-by-word until we gain a complete understanding of some the finest works of contemporary art.

You May Also Like:
Switch On Pop, Broken Record, The Nod, Watching The Throne

CLUBLIFE
Host: DJ Tiësto
Frequency: Weekly
Average Show Length: 60 Minutes

Description:
Subscribe to CLUBLIFE by Tiësto for an hour of the best club tracks

from around the world with your favorite DJ.

You May Also Like:
AVICII FM, Spinnin' Sessions, Hardwell On Air Official Podcast,A State of Trance Official Podcast, Above & Beyond: Group Therapy

Mogul: The Life and Death of Chris Lighty
Host: Reggie Osse
Frequency: Weekly
Average Show Length: 30 Minutes

Description:
Chris Lighty was a giant in hip-hop. He managed Foxy Brown, Fat Joe, Missy Elliott, Busta Rhymes, LL Cool J, 50 Cent—anyone who was anyone worked with Lighty. But in 2012 he was found dead at his home in the Bronx, a death that left the music world reeling. In this podcast miniseries from Gimlet Media and Loud Speakers Network, we tell the story of Chris Lighty, from the first breakbeat to the last heartbeat.

You May Also Like:
Ear Hustle, The Combat Jack Show, Sworn, Drink Champs, Reveal

Tiny Desk Concerts
Host: Bob Boilen
Frequency: Daily
Average Show Length: 20 Minutes

Description:
Tiny Desk Concerts from NPR Music feature your favorite musicians performing at All Songs Considered host Bob Boilen's desk in the NPR office. Hear Wilco, Adele, Passion Pit, Tinariwen, Miguel, The xx and many more.

You May Also Like:
Song Exploder, Sound Opinions, KEXP Song of the Day, KEXP Live Performances Podcast, KEXP Presents Music That Matters

Switched On Pop
Host: Nate Sloan
Frequency: Weekly
Average Show Length: 45 Minutes

Description:
Pop music surrounds us, but how often do we really listen to what we're hearing? Switched on Pop is the podcast that pulls back the curtain on pop music. Each episode, join musicologist Nate Sloan and songwriter Charlie Harding as they reveal the secret formulas that make pop songs so infectious. By figuring out how pop hits work their magic, you'll fall in love with songs you didn't even know you liked.

You May Also Like:
And The Writer Is...with Ross Golan, Pitch, Dissect - A Serialized Music Podcast, Popcast, Song Exploder

The Sleeping At Last Podcast
Host: Ryan O'Neal
Frequency: BiWeekly
Average Show Length: 60 Minutes

Description:
Welcome to The Sleeping At Last Podcast! My name's Ryan O'Neal, I make music under the name "Sleeping At Last." Nice to meet you! This podcast is an evolution of my ongoing series of "How It Was Made" blog posts, in which I dissect and explain how my songs take shape, one song at a time. In this podcast, I'll be talking about my creative process, the intention and thought behind my songs - what they mean to me and why I did what I did. I'll also debut some new songs on here!

You May Also Like:
Fun Therapy, Typology, The Brilliance Podcast, Sounds Good with Branden Harvey, The Road Back to You: Looking at Life Through the Lens of the Enneagram

Rosenberg Radio
Host: Peter Rosenberg
Frequency: Daily
Average Show Length: 60 Minutes

Description:
Between Real Late, Ebro in the Morning, The Michael Kay Show,
Cheap Heat, and Bite the Mic there is plenty of Rosenbergcontent to
go around.

You May Also Like:
Datt's What She Said, Improper Etiquette, ENN with Peter Rosenberg,
Ebro In The Morning on HOT 97, The Premium Pete Show

Above & Beyond: Group Therapy
Host: Various
Frequency: Weekly
Average Show Length: 60 Minutes

Description:
Group Therapy is the weekly radio show from Above & Beyond also
known as ABGT.

You May Also Like:
Hardwell On Air Official Podcast, A State of Trance Official Podcast,
CLUBLIFE, Gareth Emery: Electric For Life , AVICII FM

Off Book: The Improvised Musical
Hosts: Jessica McKenna, Zach Reino
Frequency: Weekly
Average Show Length: 60 Minutes

Description:
It takes years for a Broadway musical to hit the stage, but on OFF
BOOK: The Improvised Musical, you get a brand new original
musical every week!

You May Also Like:
High and Mighty, Doughboys, Superego, The Hooray Show

Wheeler Walker Jr. Podcast
Host: Wheeler Walker Jr.
Frequency: Weekly
Average Show Length: 45 Minutes

Description:
King of Country Music, Wheeler Walker Jr., talks music and life with some of the biggest stars in music, comedy and society. No rules, just real talk..

You May Also Like:
Walking The Floor, This Past Weekend, Kill Tony, Bertcast's Podcast

Popcast
Hosts: Jon Pareles, Jon Caramanica
Frequency: Weekly
Average Show Length: 60 Minutes

Description:
New York Times music critics Jon Pareles and Jon Caramanica talk each week about the latest pop music news, the top songs, the best albums, the biggest stars — and the up and coming stars you haven't heard of yet.

You May Also Like:
Switched On Pop, Sound Opinions, Rolling Stone Music Now, KEXP Presents Music That Matters, Slate's Culture Gabfest

Young & Happy
Hosts: Caleb Pressley, Adam Ferrone
Frequency: Weekly
Average Show Length: 30 Minutes

Description:
Caleb Pressley is college football's first ever Supervisor of Morale. Adam Ferrone (Rone) is the two-time defending battle rap champion of the world. They're some happy guys. On Young and Happy, Caleb and Rone dive into the notion that everything humans do is predicated on our own happiness. They explore all the inner-

workings of becoming intentionally happy, while talking to people from all walks of life about what influences their daily joy.

You May Also Like:
Storyboards, KFC Radio, Zero Blog Thirty, The Podfathers, Mickstape

KEXP Song of the Day
Host: Various
Frequency: Daily
Average Show Length: 5 Minutes

Description:
KEXP's Song of the Day podcast features exclusive in-studio performances, unreleased songs, and recordings from independent musicians that KEXP thinks listeners should hear along with songs from more well-known artists.

You May Also Like:
Song of the Day, Today's Top Tune, Tiny Desk Concerts - Audio, All Songs Considered, Live In Concert from NPR's All Songs Considered

The Combat Jack Show
Host: Various
Frequency: Weekly
Average Show Length: 60 Minutes

Description:
The undisputed #1 HipHop podcast, the Combat Jack Show features interviews with HipHop icons & the most in-depth conversations about music, news, culture & race. Listen to Russell Simmons, Chuck D, Damon Dash, Rza, Scarface, D-Nice and more share personal stories and talk exclusively about their journeys, philosophies and viewpoints.

You May Also Like:
Rap Radar Podcast, Drink Champs, TK Kirkland Show, The Joe Budden Podcast, Outchea with Lil' Duval.

NEWS & POLITICS

2018 News & Politics Top Pick
The Daily
Host: Michael Barbaro
Frequency: Daily
Average Show Length: 20 Minutes

This moment demands an explanation. This show is on a mission to find it. Only what you want to know, none of what you don't. Hosted by Michael Barbaro. Powered by New York Times journalism. Twenty minutes a day, five days a week, ready by 6 a.m.

You May Also Like:
Pod Save America, Up First, NPR Politics Podcast

Kickass News
Host: Ben Mathis
Frequency: Weekly
Average Show Length: 60 Minutes

Description:
Hosted by Hollywood producer and political media strategist Ben Mathis, KickAss News is a twice weekly podcast that features the most interesting personalities and thought leaders in politics, entertainment, tech, business, science, and more.

You May Also Like:
Dream Big Podcast, Something You Should Know, Sips, Suds, & Smokes

The Uncertain Hour
Host: Krissy Clark
Frequency: Monthly
Average Show Length: 60 Minutes

Description:
In The Uncertain Hour, host Krissy Clark dives into one controversial topic each season to reveal the surprising origin stories of our economy. From the Marketplace Wealth & Poverty Desk, each season goes beyond buzzwords to bust longstanding myths and uncover surprising backstories. Because the things we fight the most about are the things we know the least about.

You May Also Like:
The Impact, The United States of Anxiety, There Goes the Neighborhood

Pod Save America
Host: Jon Favreau, Tommy Vietor, Jon Lovett, and Daniel Pfeiffer
Frequency: Weekly
Average Show Length: 90 Minutes

Description:
Four former aides to President Obama — Jon Favreau, Dan

Pfeiffer, Jon Lovett, and Tommy Vietor — are joined by journalists, politicians, comedians, and activists for a freewheeling conversation about politics, the press and the challenges posed by the Trump presidency.

You May Also Like:
The Daily, NPR Politics Podcast, Revisionist History

The Ben Shapiro Show
Host: Ben Shapiro
Frequency: Daily
Average Show Length: 60 Minutes

Description:
Podcast by The Daily Wire.

You May Also Like:
Louder With Crowder, The Rubin Report, The Mark Levin Show Podcast

Serial
Host: Sarah Koenig
Frequency: Weekly
Average Show Length: 60 Minutes

Description:
Serial is a podcast from the creators of This American Life, hosted by Sarah Koenig. Serial unfolds one story - a true story - over the course of a whole season. The show follows the plot and characters wherever they lead, through many surprising twists and turns. Sarah won't know what happens at the end of the story until she gets there, not long before you get there with her. Each week she'll bring you the latest chapter, so it's important to listen in, starting with Episode 1. New episodes are released on Thursday mornings.

You May Also Like:
Stuff You Should Know, Radiolab, TED Radio Hour

Up First
Hosts: Rachel Martin, David Greene, Steve Inskeep
Frequency: Daily
Average Show Length: 13 Minutes

Description:
NPR's Up First is the news you need to start your day. The biggest stories and ideas — from politics to pop culture — in 10 minutes. Hosted by Rachel Martin, David Greene and Steve Inskeep, with reporting and analysis from NPR News.

You May Also Like:
The Daily, Pod Save America, Radiolab Presents: More Perfect

Up and Vanished
Host: Payne Lindsey
Frequency: Weekly
Average Show Length: 50 Minutes

Description:
Up and Vanished is an investigative podcast that explores the unsolved disappearance of Georgia beauty queen and high school teacher, Tara Grinstead. The 11-year-old cold case is the largest case file in the history of Georgia. Follow along as host Payne Lindsey, a film director turned amateur investigator, examines old case evidence and re-interviews persons of interest. What happened to Tara Grinstead?

You May Also Like:
In the Dark, Accused, Someone Knows Something

Someone Knows Something
Hosts: Charles Moore, Henry Dee
Frequency: Monthly
Average Show Length: 60 Minutes

Description:
In 1964, the remains of Charles Moore and Henry Dee were found in the Mississippi River. But no one was convicted. 40 years later,

Charles's brother Thomas returns to Mississippi with David Ridgen to reopen the case and confront the Klan.

You May Also Like:
In the Dark, Accused, Up and Vanished

PR Politics Podcast
Host: Scott Detrow
Frequency: Weekly
Average Show Length: 35 Minutes

Description:
With weekly roundups and quick takes on news of the day, you don't have to keep up with politics to know what's happening. You just have to keep up with us.

You May Also Like:
Pod Save America, The Daily, FiveThirtyEight Politics

FiveThirty Eight Politics
Host: Nate Silve
Frequency: Weekly
Average Show Length: 45 Minutes

Description:
Nate Silver and the FiveThirtyEight team cover the latest in politics, tracking the issues and "game-changers" every week.

You May Also Like:
Keepin' it 1600, Vox's The Weeds, NPR Politics Podcast

Lovett or Leave It
Host: Jon Lovett
Frequency: Weekly
Average Show Length: 75 Minutes

Description:
Comedians, actors, journalists, and many, many renowned Friends of the Pod for a roundup of the week's top news. Rants! Games!

Global News Podcast
Host: Various
Frequency: Daily
Average Show Length: 30 Minutes

Description:
The day's top stories from BBC News compiled twice daily in the week, once at weekends.

You May Also Like:
The Economist Radio (All audio), English as a Second Language (ESL) Podcast - Learn English Online, NPR Politics Podcast

Stay Tuned with Preet – WNYC, CAFE and Pineapple
Host: Preet Bharara
Frequency: Weekly
Average Show Length: 50 Minutes

Description:
Join Preet Bharara, the former U.S. Attorney who fought corruption, financial fraud and violent crime, in a podcast about justice and fairness.

You May Also Like:
Crooked Conversations, Majority 54, With Friends Like These

Crimetown
Hosts: Marc Smerling, Zac Stuart-Pontier
Frequency: Weekly
Average Show Length: 30 Minutes

Description:
Welcome to Crimetown, a new series from Gimlet Media and the creators of HBO's The Jinx. Every season, we'll investigate the culture of crime in a different American city.

You May Also Like:
Up and Vanished, In the Dark, Accused

NPR News Now
Host: Susan Stamberg
Frequency: Hourly
Average Show Length: 5 Minutes

Description:
The latest news in five minutes.

You May Also Like:
PBS NewsHour – Segments, NBC Nightly News, Global News Podcast

True Crime Garage
Host: Nic and the Captain
Frequency: Weekly
Average Show Length: 90 Minutes

Description:
Each week Nic and the Captain fire up the true crime garage flying ship fueled with beer, great discussion and listener participation. The garage covers a new case each week from headline news to local real life horror stories.

You May Also Like:
The Generation Why Podcast, Unsolved Murders: True Crime Stories, Casefile True Crime

MSNBC Rachel Maddow
Host: Rachel Maddow
Frequency: Daily
Average Show Length: 45 Minutes

Description:
Rachel Maddow provides in-depth reporting to illuminate the current state of political affairs and reveals the importance of transparency and accountability from our leaders.

You May Also Like:
Real Time with Bill Maher, Slate's Political Gabfest, The Axe Files

Pod Save the World
Host: Tommy Vietor
Frequency: Weekly
Average Show Length: 45 Minutes

Description:
"Pod Save America" cohost Tommy Vietor thought foreign policy was boring and complicated until he got the education of a lifetime working for President Obama's National Security Council. His new show "Pod Save the World" will bring you behind the scenes into White House Situation Room meetings and secret negotiations through a series of conversations with people who were there.

You May Also Like:
Keepin' it 1600, FiveThirtyEight Politics, Vox's The Weeds

The Takeout
Host: Major Garrett
Frequency: Weekly
Average Show Length: 45 Minutes

Description:
Politics, policy and a side of pop culture: Major Garrett and company serve up a balanced diet of serious discussion, humor and food...for thought.

You May Also Like:
Bob Schieffer's "About the News" with H. Andrew Schwartz, Powerhouse Politics, Reliable Sources with Brian Stelter

In the Dark
Host: APM Reports
Frequency: Weekly
Average Show Length: 45 Minutes

Description:
Child abductions are rare crimes. And they're typically solved. For 27 years, the investigation into the abduction of Jacob Wetterling in rural Minnesota yielded no answers. In the most comprehensive

reporting on this case, APM Reports and reporter Madeleine Baran reveal how law enforcement mishandled one of the most notorious child abductions in the country and how those failures fueled national anxiety about stranger danger, led to the nation's sex-offender registries and raise questions about crime-solving effectiveness and accountability.

You May Also Like:
Accused, Someone Knows Something, Up and Vanished

Pod Save the People
Host: DeRay Mckesson
Frequency: Weekly
Average Show Length: 80 Minutes

Description:
Organizer and activist DeRay Mckesson takes you inside conversations about culture, social justice, and politics by exploring the history, language, and people who are shaping the struggle for progress — and talking about the steps that each of us can take to make a difference.

You May Also Like:
Keepin' it 1600, Vox's The Weeds, The Axe Files with David Axelrod

Louder With Crowder
Host: Steven Crowder
Frequency: Weekly
Average Show Length: 90 Minutes

Description:
Steven Crowder brings you news, entertainment and politics with the most politically incorrect show on the web. Guests, rants, sketches, your calls ... it's whatever.

You May Also Like:
The Ben Shapiro Show, The Andrew Klavan Show, The Rubin Report

The Axe Files with David Axelrod
Host: David Axelrod
Frequency: Weekly
Average Show Length: 90 Minutes

Description:
David Axelrod, the founder and director of the University of Chicago Institute of Politics, brings you The Axe Files, a series of revealing interviews with key figures in the political world. Go beyond the soundbites and get to know some of the most interesting players in politics.

You May Also Like:
Keepin' it 1600, FiveThirtyEight Politics, Pod Save the World

Majority 54
Host: Jason Kander
Frequency: Weekly
Average Show Length: 60 Minutes

Description:
Jason Kander is an army veteran from Kansas City, Missouri and the first millennial elected to statewide office in the United States. He's traveling the country to help the 54% of us who didn't vote for Donald Trump talk to those of us who did about the most divisive issues in our country.

You May Also Like:
Stay Tuned with Preet, Keepin' it 1600, The New Washington

A Killing On the Cape
Host: Mark Remillard
Frequency: Weekly
Average Show Length: 45 Minutes

Description:
It was a crime that rocked an idyllic seaside town in Cape Cod -- the 2002 murder of Christa Worthington, who was found stabbed to death with her 2-year-old daughter, unharmed at her side. What

came next was a three-year search for her killer that would involve unorthodox steps by police, a lengthy list of potential suspects, and an entire town under suspicion. Christa's trash collector, Christopher McCowen, would eventually be convicted of the crime, but his trial would raise questions about the evidence, investigative methods, and whether racial prejudice played a role.

You May Also Like:
Accused, Young Charlie by Hollywood & Crime, Heaven's Gate

1A
Host: Joshua Johnson
Frequency: Daily
Average Show Length: 30 Minutes

Description:
1A champions America's right to speak freely. News with those who make the news, great guests and topical debate. Weekday conversation framed in ways to make you think, share and engage.

You May Also Like:
Diane Rehm: On My Mind, Can He Do That?, On the Media

Accused
Host: Various
Frequency: Weekly
Average Show Length: 45 Minutes

Description:
Season 2: A soft-hearted prison minister was found killed in her Kentucky apartment, and Newport police zeroed in on an ex-convict she'd counseled. Thirty years later, the conviction is overturned and the case is once again unsolved. The Cincinnati Enquirer investigates: Was William Virgil wrongly convicted for murder? Season 1: When Elizabeth Andes was found murdered in her Ohio apartment in 1978, police and prosecutors decided within hours it was an open-and-shut case. Two juries disagreed. The Cincinnati Enquirer investigates: Was the right guy charged, or did a killer walk free?

RELIGION & SPIRITUALITY

2018 Religion & Spirituality Top Pick
Elevation Church Podcast
Host: Pastor Steven Furtick
Frequency: Weekly
Average Show Length: 30 Minutes

The weekly podcast of Elevation Church led by
Pastor Steven Furtick.

You May Also Like:
Bethel Church Sermon of the Week, Churchome
with Judah Smith, Elevation Church Podcast, Craig
Groeschel Leadership Podcast,
Brian Houston Podcast

Are You Real | Finding Your Purpose | Discover Your Talents | Christianity | Christian | Believer | Faith | Christ Follower
Host: Jon B. Fuller
Frequency: Weekly
Average Show Length: 60 Minutes

Description:
Jon Fuller is on a mission to be a true example of Christ in his life and in his work. He introduces you to men and women of faith who have walked different paths to find a true Christianity that they live out each and every day. Some paths have been bumpy and filled with debris, but through it all, grace and faith have been a sustaining force in the lives of these men and women. You won't find any fake and phoney Christianity here.....just real people with a heart for God and living out His call on their lives.

You May Also Like:
Stand Up Speak Up, Sips, Suds, & Smokes, Thaddeus Ellenburg's Casual Friday, Jim Beaver's Project Action, Flipping Houses for Rookies

Joel Osteen Podcast
Host: Joel Osteen
Frequency: Weekly
Average Show Length: 30 Minutes

Description:
Welcome to the weekly audio Podcast from Joel Osteen. Joel and Victoria Osteen are pastors of Lakewood Church in Houston, Texas, a vibrant and diverse church that Forbes calls the largest and fastest - growing congregation in America.

You May Also Like:
The Potter's Touch, Joyce Meyer Radio Podcast, Joyce Meyer TV Audio Podcast, Joyce Meyer Ministries TV Podcast, The Potter's Touch

Legacy-Dads Podcast
Host: Various
Frequency: Weekly
Average Show Length: 30 Minutes

Description:
Legacy Dads started in 2005 as a journal of one man's journey to become a better Christian man, husband, and father. In 2017, Legacy Dads has 60,000+ followers and empowers men to be the spiritual leaders of their families and take an active role in their faith.

You May Also Like:
Brick By Brick, No Parking, BWWF Podcast, Sucks Radio

The Liturgists Podcast
Host: Michaek Gungor, Mike McHargue, Lissa Paino
Frequency: BiWeekly
Average Show Length: 60 Minutes

Description:
Michael Gungor and Science Mike host a conversation about the beauty and tragedy of human existence.

You May Also Like:
Ask Science Mike, The RobCast, The BadChristian Podcast, The Road Back to You: Looking at Life Through the Lens of the Enneagram, The Bible For Normal People

The RobCast
Host: Rob Bell
Frequency: Weekly
Average Show Length: 60 Minutes

Description:
The RobCast is a weekly podcast by Rob Bell

You May Also Like:
Ask Science Mike, The Liturgists Podcast, Magic Lessons with Elizabeth Gilbert, Riverhead Books, Homilies

Christ is the Cure
Host: Nick Campbell
Frequency: Weekly
Average Show Length: 60 Minutes

Description:
Dedicated to bringing back orthodox Christianity (not to be confused with the Greek church), interest in theology, and the application of said theology.

You May Also Like:
South of the 6ix, Dialectable Pod, Charles Ortleb's Truth to Power

Mindful Living Spiritual Awakening
Host: Marijo Puleo PhD
Frequency: BiWeekly
Average Show Length: 60 Minutes

Description:
For people interested in mindfulness and meditation and experiencing aspects of spiritual awakening. Learn practical ways to meditate; explore your intuitive talents; helpful life skills; and science that supports these experiences.

You May Also Like:
The Positive Head Podcast, My Seven Chakras, The Energy Healing Podcast, Law of Attraction Secrets, Daily Meditation Podcast

Crazy Love Podcast
Host: Francis Chan
Frequency: Weekly
Average Show Length: 60 Minutes

Description:
Audio Podcast with Francis Chan, best-selling author of Crazy Love, Forgotten God, Erasing Hell, Multiply, and You and Me Forever.

You May Also Like:
John Piper Sermons, The Bible Project

Tara Brach
Host: Tara Brach
Frequency: Weekly
Average Show Length: 60 Minutes

Description:
Tara Brach is a leading western teacher of Buddhist (mindfulness) meditation, emotional healing and spiritual awakening.

You May Also Like:
Good Life Project, On Being with Krista Tippett, Sounds True: Insights at the Edge, The One You Feed, 10% Happier with Dan Harris

Joyce Meyer Radio Podcast
Host: Joyce Meyer
Frequency: Weekly
Average Show Length: 60 Minutes

Description:
Enjoying Everyday Life® is a daily TV and radio broadcast provided by Joyce Meyer Ministries.

You May Also Like:
Joel Osteen Podcast, The Potter's Touch, Daily Radio Program with Charles Stanley - In Touch Ministries, Pastor Rick's Daily Hope, Elevation Church Podcast

The Bible Project
Host: Tim Mackie & Jon Collins
Frequency: Weekly
Average Show Length: 60 Minutes

Description:
The creators of The Bible Project have in-depth conversations about the Bible, theology, and history. A companion podcast to The Bible Project videos found on youtube.com/thebibleproje

You May Also Like:
Crazy Love Podcast, TGC Podcast, Ask Pastor John

For The Love With Jen Hatmaker Podcast
Host: Jen Hatmaker
Frequency: Weekly
Average Show Length: 60 Minutes

Description:
"For the love" of...People. Home. Stories. Shoes. Family. Jesus. Community. TV. Travel. Food. Culture. The hilarious best-selling author and star of HGTV's "My Big Family Renovation" invites you to drop by and catch up with her friends as they laugh and chat about all the things we love.

You May Also Like:
The Shauna Niequist Podcast, The Happy Hour with Jamie Ivey, That Sounds Fun with Annie F. Downs, God Centered Mom Podcast, Glorious in the Mundane Podcast with Christy Nockels

Timothy Keller Sermons Podcast by Gospel in Life
Host: Timothy Keller
Frequency: Weekly
Average Show Length: 60 Minutes

Description:
Classic sermons by Tim Keller, Pastor of Redeemer Presbyterian Church in New York City and NY Times best-selling author of "The Reason for God: Belief in an Age of Skepticism."

You May Also Like:
John Piper Sermons, The Village Church - Sermons, TGC Podcast, Crazy Love Podcast, Ask Pastor John

Building Relationships
Host: Dr. Gary Chapman
Frequency: Weekly
Average Show Length: 60 Minutes

Description:
The weekly One-Hour Program from Moody Publishers and Moody Broadcasting.

Pray As You Go
Host: Various
Frequency: Daily
Average Show Length: 10 Minutes

Description:
Pray-as-you-go brings together music, a passage of scripture and a few questions for personal reflection in a new 10-13 minute prayer session every day. Produced by the British Jesuits.

You May Also Like:
Catholic Stuff You Should Know, UMD NEWMAN CATHOLIC CAMPUS MINISTRY, The Word on Fire Show - Catholic Faith and Culture, Bishop Robert Barron's Sermons - Catholic Preaching and Homilies, Homilies.

Craig Groeschel Leadership Podcast
Host: Life.Church: Craig Groesche
Frequency: Monthly
Average Show Length: 15 Minutes

Description:
A conversation designed to help you make the most of your potential as you work to become the leader God created you to be.

You May Also Like:
Life.Church: Craig Groeschel Audio, Andy Stanley Leadership Podcast, The Carey Nieuwhof Leadership Podcast: Lead Like Never Before, Elevation Church Podcast, Churchome with Judah Smith

Let My People Think
Host: Ravi Zacharias
Frequency: Weekly
Average Show Length: 30 Minutes

Description:
Let My People Think with Ravi Zacharias is a 30-minute radio program from Ravi Zacharias International Ministries that powerfully mixes biblical teaching and Christian apologetics.

Exploring My Strange Bible
Host: Tim Mackie
Frequency: Weekly
Average Show Length: 60 Minutes

Description:
Download past episodes or subscribe to future episodes of
Exploring My Strange Bible by Tim Mackie, Pastor, Professor, Lead
Theologian and Co-founder of The Bible Project, for free.

You May Also Like:
The Bible Project, Tim Mackie Sermons, Bridgetown Audio Podcast,
The Bible For Normal People, Pray the Word with David Platt

Fresh Life Church
Host: Pastor Levi Lusko
Frequency: Weekly
Average Show Length: 60 Minutes

Description:
This is the podcast of the teachings of Fresh Life Church in Kalispell
Montana with Pastor Levi Lusko.

You May Also Like:
VOUS Church, Zoe Church LA, fresh life church, Passion City Church
Podcast, Churchome with Judah Smith

Harry Potter and the Sacred Text
Host: Vanessa Zoltan, Casper ter Kuile & Ariana Nedelman
Frequency: Weekly
Average Show Length: 60 Minutes

Description:
It's the English class you didn't know you missed and the meaningful
conversations you didn't know you craved. Join Vanessa Zoltan and
Casper ter Kuile as they bring thought, reflection and laughter to
Harry Potter; not just as novels, but as instructive and inspirational
texts that will teach us about our own lives. Relive the magic chapter
by chapter as they explore themes such as commitment, revenge

and forgiveness. This podcast creates time in your week to think about life's big questions. Because reading fiction doesn't just help us escape the world, it helps us live in it.

You May Also Like:
Gilmore Guys, The Bright Sessions, Myths and Legends, MuggleCast: the Harry Potter podcast, PotterCast - The Harry Potter Podcasts

Bethel Church Sermon of the Week
Host: Bethel Church Redding
Frequency: Weekly
Average Show Length:60 Minutes

Description:
Bethel Church is a community of believers led by pastor Bill Johnson in Redding, California. We are passionate about God and people. Our mission is revival: the personal, regional, and global expansion of God's Kingdom through his manifest presence.

You May Also Like:
Kris Vallotton's Podcast, Elevation Church Podcast, Brian Houston Podcast, Conversations with John & Lisa Bevere, Jesus Culture Podcasts

The Potter's Touch
Host: Bishop T.D. Jakes
Frequency: Weekly
Average Show Length: 60 Minutes

Description:
The Potter's Touch, a weekly program, with Bishop T.D. Jakes, tackles today's topics and confronts the hidden issues and invisible scars that go untreated. This broadcast carries healing and restoration into homes of hurting people, unearthing taboo topics and offering practical and spiritual solutions to life's toughest questions.

You May Also Like:
Joel Osteen Podcast, Joyce Meyer TV Audio Podcast

The Village Church - Sermons
Host: The Village Church
Frequency: Weekly
Average Show Length: 60 Minutes

Description:
The Village Church exists to bring glory to God by making disciples through gospel-centered worship, gospel-centered community, gospel-centered service and gospel-centered multiplication.

You May Also Like:
Timothy Keller Sermons Podcast by Gospel in Life, John Piper Sermons, Crazy Love Podcast, Mark Driscoll Audio, TGC Podcast

Girls Night
Host: Stephanie May Wilson
Frequency: Weekly
Average Show Length: 15 Minutes

Description:
Each week on the podcast, I have a girlfriend over and we talk through one of the biggest questions we have about our lives as women. We're talking about friendship, faith, relationships, and self-confidence, about our callings in life and how to live our lives to the absolute full. Life is so much better, easier, and absolutely more fun when we navigate it together as girlfriends, and that's exactly what we'll be doing each week in the podcast! About Stephanie: Stephanie May Wilson is an author, blogger, speaker, and best friend writing about the kinds of things you'd talk about with your best friends at a girls night. She believes in the healing power of a great cup of coffee, real-talk with best friends, and that even a random Tuesday is perfect for a champagne toast.

You May Also Like:
Give Grace Podcast, Love That Lasts with Jefferson & Alyssa Bethke, Journeywomen, Dear Daughters, Uniquely Woman

Your Move with Andy Stanley Podcast
Host: Andy Stanley
Frequency: Weekly
Average Show Length: 60 Minutes

Description:
Welcome to the Your Move with Andy Stanley podcast. In this weekly 30-minute message from Andy, you will discover how to make better decisions and live with fewer regrets.

You May Also Like:
Andy Stanley Leadership Podcast, North Point Community Church, Daily Radio Program with Charles Stanley - In Touch Ministries, Elevation Church Podcast, The Village Church — Sermons

Oh No Ross and Carrie
Host: Ross Blocher, Carrie Poppy
Frequency: Weekly
Average Show Length: 60 Minutes

Description:
Welcome to Oh No, Ross and Carrie!, the show where we don't just report on fringe science, spirituality, and claims of the paranormal, but take part ourselves.

You May Also Like:
The McElroy Brothers Will Be In Trolls 2, Til Death Do Us Blart, Wonderful!, CoolGames Inc, Throwing Shade

John Piper Sermons
Host: Desiring God
Frequency: BiWeekly
Average Show Length: 60 Minutes

Description:
John Piper is founder and teacher of desiringGod.org.

You May Also Like:
Ask Pastor John, Timothy Keller Sermons Podcast , LifeThe Village

SCIENCE & MEDICINE

2018 Science & Medicine Top Pick
Hidden Brain
Host: Shankar Vedantam
Frequency: Weekly
Average Show Length: 30 Minutes

The Hidden Brain helps curious people understand the world — and themselves. Using science and storytelling, Hidden Brain's host Shankar Vedantam reveals the unconscious patterns that drive human behavior, the biases that shape our choices, and the triggers that direct the course of our relationships.

You May Also Like:
Revisionist History, Freakonomics Radio, Radiolab,
Stuff You Should Know,
Radiolab Presents: More Perfect.

Radiolab
Host: Jad Abumrad, Robert Krulwich
Frequency: Weekly
Average Show Length: 60 Minutes

Description:
A two-time Peabody Award-winner, Radiolab is an investigation told through sounds and stories, and centered around one big idea. In the Radiolab world, information sounds like music and science and culture collide.
You May Also Like:
This American Life, Invisibilia, TED Radio Hour, The Moth, S-Town

Sword and Scale
Host: Mike Boudet
Frequency: Weekly
Average Show Length: 60 Minutes

Description:
The Sword and Scale true-crime podcast is an immersive audio experience covering the underworld of criminal activity and the demented minds that perform the most despicable and unthinkable actions, proving that the worst monsters are very real. We cover true-crime stories, high-profile trials, unsolved murders and missing persons cases.

You May Also Like:
Casefile True Crime, My Favorite Murder with Karen Kilgariff and Georgia Hardstark, True Crime Garage, Someone Knows Something, Up and Vanished

Invisibilia
Host: NPR
Frequency: Weekly

Description:
Invisibilia (Latin for invisible things) is about the invisible forces that control human behavior – ideas, beliefs, assumptions and emotions. Co-hosted by Hanna Rosin, Alix Spiegel, and Lulu Miller, Invisibilia

interweaves narrative storytelling with scientific research that will ultimately make you see your own life differently.

You May Also Like:
Radiolab, Revisionist History, 99% Invisible, This American Life, Radiolab Presents: More Perfect

Waking Up with Sam Harris

Host: Sam Harris
Frequency: Weekly
Average Show Length: 90 Minutes

Description:
Join neuroscientist, philosopher, and best-selling author Sam Harris as he explores important and controversial questions about the human mind, society, and current events.

You May Also Like:
StarTalk Radio, Common Sense with Dan Carlin, Dan Carlin's Hardcore History, The Tim Ferriss Show, The Joe Rogan Experience

Ridiculous History

Hosts: Zach Levy, Michael Brown
Frequency: Weekly
Average Show Length: 60 Minutes

Description:
Did San Diego fall victim to a real-life weather manipulating supervillain? What on Earth are Soviet bone records? Each week, longtime friends and veteran podcasters Ben Bowlin and Noel Brown dive into some of the weirdest stories from across the span of human civilization in Ridiculous History.

You May Also Like:
HowStuffWorks NOW, What Really Happened?, Why We Eat What We Eat, Historical Figures, Haunted Places

StarTalk Radio
Host: Neil deGrasse Tyson
Frequency: Daily
Average Show Length: 60 Minutes

Description:
Science meets comedy and pop culture on StarTalk Radio!
Astrophysicist and Hayden Planetarium director Neil deGrasse
Tyson, his comic co-hosts, guest celebrities and scientists discuss
astronomy, physics, and everything else about life in the universe.

You May Also Like:
*The Nerdist, Dan Carlin's Hardcore History, Waking Up with Sam
Harris, The Joe Rogan Experience, Radiolab*

Science Vs
Host: Wendy Zukerman
Frequency: Weekly
Average Show Length: 30 Minutes

Description:
There are a lot of fads, blogs and strong opinions, but then there's
SCIENCE. Science Vs is the show from Gimlet Media that finds out
what's fact, what's not, and what's somewhere in between. We do
the hard work of sifting through all the science so you don't have to.

You May Also Like:
*Radiolab Presents: More Perfect, Science Vs, Embedded, Reveal,
Invisibilia*

DONE DISAPPEARED
Host: John David Booter
Frequency: Weekly
Average Show Length: 10 Minutes

Description:
From John David Booter, this is DONE DISSAPEARED: A True Crime
Podcast by JOHN DAVID BOOTER. New episodes every Wednesday

Stuff To Blow Your Mind
Host: Christian Sager, Robert Lamb, Joe McCormick
Frequency: Weekly
Average Show Length: 90 Minutes

Description:
Deep in the back of your mind, you've always had the feeling that there's something strange about reality. There is. Join Robert, Joe and Christian as they examine neurological quandaries, cosmic mysteries, evolutionary marvels and our transhuman future.

You May Also Like:
How To Do Everything, StarTalk Radio, Myths and Legends, Science Friday, Science Vs.

TEDTalks Science and Medicine
Host: Various
Frequency: Weekly
Average Show Length: 15 Minutes

Description:
Some of the world's greatest scientists, doctors and medical researchers share their discoveries and visions onstage at the TED conference, TEDx events and partner events around the world.

You May Also Like:
Science Friday, Science Magazine Podcast, Stuff To Blow Your Mind, Comedy Central Stand-Up, BrainStuff

Science Friday
Host: Ira Flatow
Frequency: Weekly
Average Show Length: 45 Minutes

Description:
Brain fun for curious people.

You May Also Like:
StarTalk Radio, Science Vs, How To Do Everything

Mysterious Universe
Host: Benjamin Grundy
Frequency: Weekly
Average Show Length: 90 Minutes

Description:
Mysterious Universe brings you the latest news and podcasts covering the strange, extraordinary, weird, wonderful and everything in between.

You May Also Like:
Mysteries Abound, Astronomy Cast, Paranormal Podcast

How To Do Everything
Host: Mike Danforth and Ian Chillag
Frequency: Weekly
Average Show Length: 20 Minutes

Description:
We're half advice show, half survival guide. We answer all your questions, from how to find a date, to how to find water in the desert.

You May Also Like:
Death, Sex & Money, Science Friday, Snap Judgment, Stuff To Blow Your Mind, Stuff Mom Never Told You

You're the Expert
Host: Chris Duffy
Frequency: BiWeekly
Average Show Length: 60 Minutes

Description:
Three comedians try to guess what a leading expert does all day and learn why their research is important. You're the Expert brings academia out of the Ivory Tower and into your iPhone.

You May Also Like:
The Story Collider, Big Data Everything, Pitch, Grumpy Old Geeks

Mysterious Radio
Host: K-Town
Frequency: Weekly
Average Show Length: 60 Minutes

Description:
Fascinating discussions on all aspects of the paranormal, conspiracy theories, UFO's, cryptozoology, mysterious places, the unexplained, the occult, ancient history, true crime and more with the foremost experts, survivors & experiencers in the world. New release every Sunday night.

You May Also Like:
Those Conspiracy Guys, REAL GHOST STORIES ONLINE, Strange Matters Podcast

The Best of Coast to Coast AM
Host: George Noory
Frequency: Daily
Average Show Length: 60 Minutes

Description:
A media phenomenon, Coast to Coast AM deals with UFOs, strange occurrences, life after death, and other unexplained (and often inexplicable) phenomena.

You May Also Like:
Mysterious Radio, Classic Art Bell Podcast, Beyond the Darkness, Coast to Coast Podcasts, Open Minds UFO Radio

The X Podcast
Host: K-Town
Frequency: Weekly
Average Show Length: 60 Minutes

Description:
The X Podcast is a brand new show that shares true stories of shadowy figures, moving objects, strange voices, and terrifying experiences that have stayed with people to this very day.

You Are Not So Smart
Host: David McRaney
Frequency: BiWeekly
Average Show Length: 60 Minutes

Description:
You Are Not So Smart is a celebration of self delusion that explores topics related to cognitive biases, heuristics, and logical fallacies. David McRaney interviews scientists about their research into how the mind works, and then he eats a cookie.

You May Also Like:
Rationally Speaking, The Skeptics' Guide to the Universe, The Partially Examined Life Philosophy Podcast, Science Vs, Inquiring Minds

BrainStuff
Host: Various
Frequency: Weekly
Average Show Length: 5 Minutes

Description:
Whether the topic is popcorn or particle physics, you can count on BrainStuff to explore -- and explain -- the everyday science in the world around us.

You May Also Like:
Science Friday, How To Do Everything, Grammar Girl Quick and Dirty Tips for Better Writing, 60-Second Science, Science Vs.

The Curbsiders Internal Medicine Podcast
Hosts: Matthew Watto, Stuart Brigham, Paul Williams, Tony Sidari
Frequency: Weekly
Average Show Length: 60 Minutes

Description:
Supercharge your learning and enhance your practice with this Internal Medicine Podcast featuring board certified Internists as they interview national and international experts to bring you clinical

pearls and practice changing knowledge. Doctors Matthew Watto, Stuart Brigham, and Paul Williams deliver some knowledge food for your brain hole. No boring lectures here, just high value content and a healthy dose of humor.

You May Also Like:
Louisville Lectures Internal Medicine Lecture Series Podcast, Hospital and Internal Medicine Podcast, Annals of Internal Medicine Podcast, AFP: American Family Physician Podcast

Nifty Thrifty Dentists Podcast
Hosts: Dr. Glenn Vo, Dr. Vinh Nguyen
Frequency: BiWeekly
Average Show Length: 60 Minutes

Description:
A podcast for Dental professionals who are looking for ways to save money in the Dental Practice. It is a podcast like no other with an interesting format and great guests. Hosted by Dr. Glenn Vo and Dr. Vinh Nguyen.

You May Also Like:
Sage Flipping Secrets, South of the 6ix, Breathe Motivation

60-Second Science
Host: Steve Mirsky
Frequency: Daily
Average Show Length: 2 Minutes

Description:
Leading science journalists provide a daily minute commentary on some of the most interesting developments in the world of science. For a full-length, weekly podcast you can subscribe to Science Talk: The Podcast of Scientific American.

You May Also Like:
Discovery, Nature Podcast, 60 Minutes, Learning English for China, BBC Learning English Drama

Real Ghost Stories Online
Hosts: Tony Brueski, Jenny Brueski
Frequency: Daily
Average Show Length: 60 Minutes

Description:
A DAILY paranormal podcast filled with real ghost stories of horror, told by real people. Stories that encompass all areas of the paranormal, supernatural, demonic, ghost investigations, haunted houses, possessions, shadow people, unexplained and more.

You May Also Like:
Mysterious Radio, Jim Harold's Campfire, PARANORMAL PODCAST, Anything Ghost Show, SCARED? - Real People Tell Their True Ghost, UFO and Paranormal Stories

Astronomy Cast
Host: Fraser Cain, Dr. Pamela L. Gay
Frequency: Weekly
Average Show Length: 30 Minutes

Description:
Astronomy Cast brings you a weekly fact-based journey through the cosmos.

You May Also Like:
Mysterious Universe, Planetary Radio, The 365 Days of Astronomy, The Skeptics' Guide to the Universe, Naked Astronomy

All In The Mind - ABC Radio National
Host: Rick Rohan, Duane Beeman
Frequency: Weekly
Average Show Length: 30 Minutes

Description:
All In The Mind is Radio National's weekly foray into the mental universe, the mind, brain and behaviour - everything from addiction to artificial intelligence.

Terrestrial
Host: Ashley Ahearn
Frequency: BiWeekly
Average Show Length: 30 Minutes

Description:
Terrestrial explores the choices we make in a world we have changed. Host Ashley Ahearn travels the country — from ranches in Oregon to churches in Colorado — to bring listeners stories about people making personal choices in the face of environmental change.

You May Also Like:
Warm Regards, Showcase from Radiotopia, Outside/In, How's Your Day?, Very Bad Words

Paranormal Podcast
Host: Jim Harold
Frequency: Weekly
Average Show Length: 60 Minutes

Description:
America's Top Paranormal Podcaster interviews the best known names in the paranormal about UFOs, Ghosts, Bigfoot, and everything paranormal!

You May Also Like:
Mysterious Universe, Mysterious Radio, REAL GHOST STORIES ONLINE, Anything Ghost Show

The Skeptics' Guide to the Universe
Host: Dr. Steven Novella
Frequency: Weekly
Average Show Length: 60 Minutes

Description:
The Skeptics' Guide to the Universe is a weekly science podcast discussing the latest science news, critical thinking, bad science, conspiracies and controversies.

SOCIETY & CULTURE

2018 Society & Culture Top Pick
Stuff You Should Know
Host: Chuck Bryant, Josh Clark
Frequency: Weekly
Average Show Length: 60 Minutes

How do landfills work? How do mosquitos work?
Join Josh and Chuck as they explore the Stuff You
Should Know about everything from genes to the
Galapagos in this podcast from HowStuffWorks.com

You May Also Like:
TED Radio Hour, This American Life, TED Talks Daily

This American Life
Host: Ira Glass
Frequency: Weekly
Average Show Length: 60 Minutes

Description:
This American Life is a weekly public radio show, heard by 2.2 million people on more than 500 stations. Another 2.5 million people download the weekly podcast. It is hosted by Ira Glass, produced in collaboration with Chicago Public Media, delivered to stations by PRX The Public Radio Exchange, and has won all of the major broadcasting awards.

You May Also Like:
Radiolab, TED Radio Hour, Stuff You Should Know

Dirty John
Host: Christopher Goffard
Frequency: Daily
Average Show Length: 40 Minutes

Description:
Debra Newell is a successful interior designer. She meets John Meehan, a handsome man who seems to check all the boxes: attentive, available, just back from a year in Iraq with Doctors Without Borders. But her family doesn't like John, and they get entangled in an increasingly complex web of love, deception, forgiveness, denial, and ultimately, survival.

You May Also Like:
Up and Vanished, Someone Knows Something

S-Town
Host: Brian Reed
Frequency: Monthly
Average Show Length: 30 Minutes

Description:
S-Town is a new podcast from Serial and This American Life, hosted

by Brian Reed, about a man named John who despises his Alabama town and decides to do something about it.

You May Also Like:
Revisionist History, Radiolab, Invisibilia, Stuff You Should Know

Where Should We Begin? with Esther Perel
Host: Esther Perel
Frequency: Weekly
Average Show Length: 45 Minutes

Description:
Step into iconic relationship therapist Esther Perel's office and listen as 10 anonymous couples in search of insight bare the raw, intimate, and profound details of their story. From infidelity, to sexlessness, to loss, it's a space for people to be heard and understood. It's also a place for us to listen and feel empowered in our own relationships.

You May Also Like:
Dear Sugars, Terrible Thanks For Asking, Modern Love, Heavyweight

Slow Burn: A Podcast About Watergate
Host: Leon Neyfakh
Frequency: Weekly
Average Show Length: 30 Minutes

Description:
You think you know the story, or maybe you don't. But Watergate was stranger, wilder, and more exciting than you can imagine. What did it feel like to live through the scandal that brought down President Nixon? Find out on this eight-episode podcast miniseries hosted by Leon Neyfakh.

You May Also Like:
The Impact, Nerdcast , The Lawfare Podcast, Off Message

Freakonomics Radio
Host: Stephen J. Dubner
Frequency: Weekly
Average Show Length: 50 Minutes

Description:
Have fun discovering the hidden side of everything with host
Stephen J. Dubner, co-author of the best-selling "Freakonomics"
books. Each week, hear surprising conversations that explore the
riddles of everyday life and the weird wrinkles of human nature—
from cheating and crime to parenting and sports.

You May Also Like:
Planet Money, Stuff You Should Know, Revisionist History

Dan Carlin's Hardcore History
Host: Dan Carlin
Frequency: Annualy
Average Show Length: 360 Minutes

Description:
Was Alexander the Great as bad a person as Adolf Hitler? What
would Apaches with modern weapons be like? Will our modern
civilization ever fall like civilizations from past eras? This isn't
academic history (and Carlin isn't a historian) but the podcast's
unique blend of high drama, masterful narration and Twilight Zone-
style twists has entertained millions of listeners.

You May Also Like:
The Joe Rogan , Revisionist History , Radiolab

Oprah's SuperSoul Conversations
Host: Oprah Winfrey
Frequency: Weekly
Average Show Length: 40 Minutes

Description:
Awaken, discover and connect to the deeper meaning of the world
around you with SuperSoul. Hear Oprah's personal selection of

her interviews with thought-leaders, best-selling authors, spiritual luminaries, as well as health and wellness experts.

Stuff You Missed in History Class
Host: Deblina Chakraborty
Frequency: Twice a Week
Average Show Length: 40 Minutes

Description:
Join Holly and Tracy as they bring you the greatest and strangest Stuff You Missed In History Class.

You May Also Like:
Dan Carlin's Hardcore History, Lore, Revisionist History

Lore
Host: Aaron Mahnke
Frequency: BiWeekly
Average Show Length: 30 Minutes

Description:
Dark historical tales that fuel our modern superstitions. Each episode explores the world of mysterious creatures, tragic events, and unusual places. Because sometimes the truth is more frightening than fiction.

You May Also Like:
My Favorite Murder, Myths and Legends, The Black Tapes

Mysterious Radio
Host: E. G. Marshall
Frequency: Monthly
Average Show Length: 60 Minutes

Description:
Fascinating discussions on all aspects of the paranormal, conspiracy theories, UFO's, cryptozoology, mysterious places, the unexplained, the occult, ancient history, true crime and more with the foremost experts, survivors & experiencers in the world.

Heaven's Gate
Host: Glynn Washington
Frequency: Weekly
Average Show Length: 45 Minutes

Description:
In 1997, thirty-nine people took their own lives in an apparent mass suicide. The events captivated the media and had people across the planet asking the same question...'Why?' 20 years later, those who lost loved ones and those who still believe - tell their story.

You May Also Like:
Cults, A Killing On the Cape, A Murder On Orchard Street, Young Charlie

Omnibus
Host: John Roderick
Frequency: Weekly
Average Show Length: 60 Minutes

Description:
Twice a week, Ken Jennings and John Roderick add a new entry to the OMNIBUS, an encyclopedic reference work of strange-but-true stories that they are compiling as a time capsule for future generations.

You May Also Like:
Road Work, Do By Friday, Top Scallops, Unwound

Revisionist History
Host: Malcolm Gladwell
Frequency: Weekly
Average Show Length: 30 Minutes

Description:
Revisionist History is Malcolm Gladwell's journey through the overlooked and the misunderstood. Every episode re-examines something from the past—an event, a person, an idea, even a song—and asks whether we got it right the first time. From Panoply Media.

Because sometimes the past deserves a second chance.

You May Also Like:
S-Town, Serial, This American Life , Freakonomics Radio, Hidden Brain

Heavyweight
Host: Jonathan Goldstein
Frequency: Weekly
Average Show Length: 40 Minutes

Description:
Maybe you've laid awake imagining how it could have been, how it might yet be, but the moment to act was never right. Well, the moment is here and the podcast making it happen is Heavyweight. Join Jonathan Goldstein for road trips, thorny reunions, and difficult conversations as he backpedals his way into the past like a therapist with a time machine. From Gimlet Media.

You May Also Like:
Reveal Reveal The Center for Investigative Reporting and PRX , Embedded, Radiolab Presents: More Perfect, Love + Radio, Ear Hustle

Young and Happy – Barstool Sports
Host: Adam Ferrone
Frequency: Daily
Average Show Length: 20 Minutes

Description:
On Young and Happy, Caleb and Rone dive into the notion that everything humans do is predicated on our own happiness. They explore all the inner-workings of becoming intentionally happy, while talking to people from all walks of life about what influences their daily joy.

You May Also Like:
Storyboards,, KFC Radio, Zero Blog Thirty, The Podfathers

Something You Should Know
Host : Mike Carruthers
Frequency: BiWeekly
Average Show Length: 40 Minutes

Description:
Sometimes all it takes is one little fact or one little piece of wisdom to change your life forever. That's the purpose and the hope of "Something You Should Know." In each episode, host Mike Carruthers interviews top experts in their field to bring you fascinating information and advice to help you save time and money, advance in your career, become wealthy, improve your relationships and help you simply get more out of life.

You May Also Like:
Kickass News, Dream Big Podcast, Are You Real, Flipping Houses for Rookies

Chasing Glory with Lilian Garcia
Host: Lilian Garcia
 Frequency: Weekly
Average Show Length: 60 Minutes

Description:
Multi-talented singer/songwriter, television personality and producer, former WWE host and Spanish beauty Lilian Garcia brings the heat and unhinges the podcast world with an all-access pass to human interest stories with your favorite athletes and entertainers. "Chasing Glory with Lilian Garcia" peels back the layers and dives deep into how they got to where they are today, and the real-life challenges in making their dreams come true. It's about to get Real, Raw & Inspiring every week on "Chasing Glory with Lilian Garcia".

You May Also Like:
Dinner With The King, Heated Conversations, X-Pac 123, Regular Girls

WeHeardWhat?!
Host: Danielle Bernstein
Frequency: Monthly
Average Show Length: 40 Minutes

Description:
Podcast by Danielle Bernstein.

Casefile True Crime
Host: Various
Frequency: Weekly
Average Show Length: 60 Minutes

Description:
Fact is scarier than fiction. Casefile, a new true crime podcast.

You May Also Like:
Sword and Scale Wondery, Someone Knows Something

Family Ghosts
Host: Panoply / Sam Dingman
Frequency: Weekly
Average Show Length: 45 Minutes

Description:
In each episode of "Family Ghosts," we'll investigate the true story behind a mysterious figure whose legend has followed a family for generations. Grandmothers who were secretly jewel smugglers, uncles who led double lives, siblings who vanished without a trace... these specters cast shadows over our lives in ways that might not be immediately obvious. But we are all formed in part by our familial collections of secrets, intrigues, and myths. By engaging with each others' legends, perhaps we can see each others' realities more clearly. Hosted by Moth Grand Slam winner Sam Dingman, whose stories have been featured on Risk!, TBTL, Benjamen Walker's Theory of Everything, and The Moth Radio Hour.

You May Also Like:
Inside Psycho, Hanging, The Moonlit Road Podcast

Serial Killers
Host: William Bonin
Frequency: Weekly
Average Show Length: 30 Minutes

Description:
Every Monday, Serial Killers takes a psychological and entertaining approach to provide a rare glimpse into the mind, methods and madness of the most notorious serial killers with the hopes of better understanding their psychological profile. With the help of voice actors, we delve deep into their lives and stories.

You May Also Like:
The Generation Why Podcast, Casefile True Crime

Criminal
Host: Phoebe Judge
Frequency: Every 15 Days
Average Show Length: 30 Minutes

Description:
Criminal is a podcast about crime. Not so much the "if it bleeds, it leads," kind of crime. Something a little more complex. Stories of people who've done wrong, been wronged, and/or gotten caught somewhere in the middle. We're a proud member of Radiotopia, from PRX, a curated network of extraordinary, story-driven shows. Learn more at radiotopia.fm.

You May Also Like:
Casefile True Crim, Sword and Scale , Crimetown , Someone Knows Something , Lore

The X Podcast
Hosts: Rocky Leflore, Josh Webb
Frequency: Monthly
Average Show Length: 15 Minutes

Description:
The X Podcast is a brand new show that shares true stories of

shadowy figures, moving objects, strange voices, and terrifying experiences that have stayed with people to this very day. Oh, and it's best to listen in the dark....and alone....if you dare. Hosted by K-Town who is a a proud military veteran and part of the BombPod Media Network

You May Also Like:
3 People Like This, View From the Penalty Box

Letters From War
Host: Various
Frequency: Quarterly
Average Show Length: 20 Minutes

Description:
Hundreds of letters, written between brothers fighting in the Pacific during World War II. Almost one a day, for every day of the war. In this podcast, you'll hear the story of these brothers — the Eyde brothers — and of World War II, as told through their letters, in their own words. Bringing the letters to life are modern U.S. military veterans. At key moments in the story, we'll talk to them about how these letters compare to their own experiences — what's universal about war and what's changed. And why everyone who picks up these letters feels like the Eyde brothers become a part of their family.

The Skinny Confidential Him & Her Podcast
Hosts: Lauryn Evarts Bosstick, Michael Bosstick
Frequency: Weekly
Average Show Length: 60 Minutes

Description:
Interviews with celebrities, entrepreneurs, influencers, experts, and thought leaders. You will also hear listener and audience questions answered on a weekly basis to answer questions on health, wellness, business, branding, marketing, and relationships.

You May Also Like:
The Bitch Bible, The Balanced Blonde

Straight Up with Stassi
Host: Stassi Schroeder
Frequency: Weekly
Average Show Length: 60 Minutes

Description:
Love her or hate her, but you can't ignore the sassy, quick-witted Stassi Schroeder, star of Bravo's "Vanderpump Rules."

You May Also Like:
The Bitch, Heather Dubrow's World, Watch What Crappens

Ear Hustle
Hosts: Earlonne Woods, Antwan Williams
Frequency: BiWeekly
Average Show Length: 30 Minutes

Description:
Ear Hustle brings you stories of life inside prison, shared and produced by those living it. The podcast is a partnership between Earlonne Woods and Antwan Williams, currently incarcerated at San Quentin State Prison, and Nigel Poor, a Bay Area artist. The team works in San Quentin's media lab to produce stories that are sometimes difficult, often funny and always honest, offering a nuanced view of people living within the American prison system.

You May Also Like:
TED Radio Hour, This American Life, TED Talks Daily

Aubrey Marcus Podcast
Host: Aubrey Marcus
Frequency: Weekly
Average Show Length: 45 Minutes

Description:
We bring in world-class guests to discuss how you can support your body, turn resistance to assistance, harness the potential of your mind and emotions, and cultivate a battle tested spirituality without all the BS. But most importantly we have some fun while we do it.

SPORTS & RECREATION

2018 Sports & Recreation Top Pick
30 For 30
Host: Jody Avirgan
Frequency: Weekly
Average Show Length: 30 Minutes

Original audio documentaries and more from the makers of the acclaimed 30 for 30 series. Sports stories like you've never heard before.

You May Also Like:
Pardon My Take, The Bill Simmons Podcast, The Ringer NBA Show, Crimetown, Channel 33

Pardon My Take
Hosts: PFT Commentator, Dan Katz
Frequency: Daily
Average Show Length: 60 Minutes

Description:
On "Pardon My Take," Big Cat & PFT Commenter deliver the loudest and most correct sports takes in the history of the spoken word. Daily topics, guests, and an inability to tell what the hosts might be doing will make this your new favorite sports talk show.

You May Also Like:
KFC Radio, The Pat McAfee Show,The Bill Simmons Podcast,Zero Blog Thirty, 30 For 30 Podcasts

The Bill Simmons Podcast
Host: Bill Simmons
Frequency: Weekly
Average Show Length: 60 Minutes

Description:
HBO and The Ringer's Bill Simmons hosts the most downloaded sports podcast of all time, with a rotating crew of celebrities, athletes, and media staples, as well as mainstays like Cousin Sal, Joe House, and a slew of other friends and family members who always happen to be suspiciously available.

You May Also Like:
The Woj Pod, The Lowe Post, Jalen & Jacoby, Pardon My Take, The Herd with Colin Cowherd

Sports Gambling Radio
Host: Adam Burke
Frequency: Daily
Average Show Length: 40 Minutes

Description:
BangTheBook Radio is the industry leader in presenting sports betting information and analysis. Our radio show segments feature

some of the most profitable handicappers and sharpest analysts in the wagering markets of college football, NFL, MLB, NHL, NBA, college basketball, and UFC.

You May Also Like:
GSMC MMA Podcast, AMsecrets Podcast, The Caffeinated Sneakerhead, GSMC Fantasy Football Podcast

View From the Penalty Box (Classic Hockey Stories)
Host: Cam Connor
Frequency: Weekly
Average Show Length: 30 Minutes

Description:
In this podcast, listen to Cam share some classic hockey stories, including being one of two players to play with Wayne Gretzky and Gordie Howe, growing up with his best friend Rowdy Roddy Piper and how he saw the hockey world - his view from the penalty box.

You May Also Like:
MAGAPod, The Loudini Rock and Roll Circus, Sage Flipping Secrets, Breathe Motivation: Inspiration, Nifty Thrifty Dentists Podcast

Season Ticket
Host: Chris Gasper
Frequency: Daily
Average Show Length: 30 Minutes

Description:
Season Ticket is full of engaging talk, insightful commentary, insider information, and unfiltered conversations with those who make news on the Boston sports scene and those who report on it five days a week. Hosted by Boston Globe sports columnist Chris Gasper, in partnership with WBUR, Boston's NPR station, this daily show will make you feel closer to your favorite teams than ever before.

You May Also Like:
Boston Baseball, Boston Globe's 108 Stitches Podcast, Bob Ryan's Boston Podcast,Quick Slants - A New England Patriots Podcast

The Herd with Colin Cowherd

Host: Colin Cowherd
Frequency: Daily
Average Show Length: 120 Minutes

Description:
The Herd with Colin Cowherd is a thought-provoking, opinionated, and topic-driven journey through the top sports stories of the day.

You May Also Like:
First Take, The Bill Simmons Podcast, Golic & Wingo, PTI, Jalen & Jacoby

One Shining Podcast with Titus and Tate

Host: Titus Frazier, Tate Frazier
Frequency: Daily
Average Show Length: 60 Minutes

Description:
Two of The Ringer's most overly obsessed basketball lovers, Mark Titus and Tate Frazier, from the hoop states of Indiana and North Carolina, talk through all the many happenings in the world of college basketball and beyond!

You May Also Like:
The Bill Simmons Podcast, Channel 33, The Ringer NBA Show, Keepin' It 1600

I AM RAPAPORT: STEREO PODCAST

Host: Michael Rapaport
Frequency: Daily
Average Show Length: 60 Minutes

Description:
Actor/Director Michael Rapaport shares his strong, funny & offensive points of view on life, sports, music, film & everything in between.

You May Also Like:
KFC Radio, The Dave Portnoy Show, The Ringer NBA Show

The Jim Rome Podcast
Host: Jim Rome
Frequency: Weekly
Average Show Length: 40 Minutes

Description:
A new show. Fresh content. A different beast.

You May Also Like:
The Rich Eisen Show, Mohr Sports, View from the Cheap Seats, Mohr Stories, The Dan Patrick Show

PTI
Hosts: Tony Kornheiser, Michael Wilbon
Frequency: Daily
Average Show Length: 20 Minutes

Description:
Tony Kornheiser and Michael Wilbon face off in the nation's capital on the day's hottest topics.

You May Also Like:
The Tony Kornheiser Show, The Herd, The Bill Simmons Podcast, The Ringer NBA Show, Skip and Shannon: Undisputed

Fantasy Focus Football
Hosts: Matthew Berry, Field Yates, Stephania Bell
Frequency: Daily
Average Show Length: 60 Minutes

Description:
ESPN fantasy experts Matthew Berry, Field Yates and Stephania Bell provide daily strategy, previews and injury reports.

You May Also Like:
Fantasy Footballers - Fantasy Football Podcast, Fantasy Football Today Podcast, The Bill Simmons Podcast, FantasyPros

Jim Beaver's Project Action

Host: Jim Beaver
Frequency: Weekly
Average Show Length: 90 Minutes

Description:
Project Action is your weekly glimpse behind the scenes with some of the biggest personalities in the world today from Action Sports, MMA, Racing, Sports, Hollywood, and Music.

You May Also Like:
Stand Up Speak Up, The Down & Dirty Radio Show, Sips, Suds, & Smokes, Are You Hearing This

The Fighter & The Kid

Host: Brendan Schaub, Bryan Callen
Frequency: Weekly
Average Show Length: 120 Minutes

Description:
The Fighter & The Kid is a weekly podcast featuring UFC heavyweight Brendan Schaub, and actor/comedian Bryan Callen. It's uncut and unedited and sometimes it's just ridiculous.

You May Also Like:
Big Brown Breakdown, The Church of What's Happening Now, The MMA Hour with Ariel Helwani, UFC Unfiltered, Your Mom's House

The Lowe Post

Host: Zach Lowe
Frequency: Weekly
Average Show Length: 60 Minutes

Description:
ESPN's Zach Lowe talks to various basketball people about various basketball things.

You May Also Like:
The Woj Pod, The Starters, The Ringer NBA Show

The Ringer NBA Show
Host: Chris Vernon
Frequency: Weekly
Average Show Length: 50 Minutes

Description:
A daily breakdown of the latest story lines, trends, and important developments in the NBA. We promise to keep the Sixers and Celtics discussion to a reasonable amount ... or to at least try.

You May Also Like:
The Woj Pod, The Lowe Post, Jalen & Jacoby, The Starters, The Chronicles of Redick

South of the 6ix
Hosts: Adam Corsair, Curtis Corsair
Frequency: Weekly
Average Show Length: 60 Minutes

Description:
A weekly podcast discussing all things Toronto Raptors and Toronto Blue Jays, with a unique perspective from someone that lives south of the Canadian border.

You May Also Like:
Christ is the Cure, Nifty Thrifty Dentists Podcast, Sage Flipping Secrets, Charles Ortleb's Truth to Power, Dialectable Pod

The Dave Portnoy Show
Host: Dave Portnoy
Frequency: Weekly
Average Show Length: 60 Minutes

Description:
A weekly "best of" podcast where we deliver to you the best 60-90 min from Barstool's daily show on Sirius XM.

You May Also Like:
KFC Radio, The Pat McAfee Show, Zero Blog Thirty, Storyboards

Fantasy Footballers
Hosts: Andy Holloway, Jason Moore, Mike Wright
Frequency: Daily
Average Show Length: 60 Minutes

Description:
The expert trio break down the world of Fantasy Football with astute analysis, strong opinions, and matchup-winning advice you can't get anywhere else.

You May Also Like:
NFL Fantasy Live, Fantasy Focus Football, Fantasy Football Today Podcast, FantasyPros,, Footballguys.com

Skip and Shannon: Undisputed
Host: Skip Bayless, Shannon Sharpe, Joe Taylor
Frequency: Daily
Average Show Length: 60 Minutes

Description:
The Skip and Shannon: Undisputed podcast. Skip Bayless, Shannon Sharpe, and Joy Taylor discuss the biggest topics of the day. It's unscripted and unfiltered.

You May Also Like:
First Take, The Stephen A. Smith Show, His & Hers & SC6, Golic & Wingo, Jalen & Jacoby

The Dan Le Batrd Show with Stugotz
Hosts: Dan Le Batard, Stugotz
Frequency: Daily
Average Show Length: 60 Minutes

Description:
Dan Le Batard, Stugotz and company share their unique perspectives from Miami Beach's Clevelander Hotel.

You May Also Like:
The Woj Pod, The Herd with Colin Cowherd, The Dan Patrick Show

First Take
Hosts: Stephen A. Smith, Max Kellerman, Molly Qerim
Frequency: Daily
Average Show Length: 90 Minutes

Description:
First Take is always a heated discussion as Stephen A. Smith, Max Kellerman and guests debate about the day's top stories.

You May Also Like:
The Starters, Skip and Shannon: Undisputed, The Herd with Colin Cowherd, Speak For Yourself with Cowherd & Whitlock, The Ringer NBA Show

The Steve Austin Show - Unleashed!
Host: Steve Austin
Frequency: Weekly
Average Show Length: 90 Minutes

Description:
Live from Hollywood, CA by way of the Broken Skull Ranch, Pro Wrestling Hall of Famer, Action Movie/TV star, Steve Austin lets loose on these no-holds barred, explicit versions of the program.

You May Also Like:
Art of Wrestling, E&C's Pod of Awesomeness,, Sam Roberts Wrestling Podcast, Something to Wrestle with Bruce Prichard, Bischoff on Wrestling

Fore Play
Hosts: Trent, Riggs
Frequency: Weekly
Average Show Length: 60 Minutes

Description:
"Fore Play" is a weekly podcast by common golfers, for common golfers. Trent, Riggs and their wide variety of guests talk about everything golf like normal folks sitting at a bar watching coverage, venting about the game's difficulties, and weighing in on pro gossip.

Laces Out
Hosts: Pat McAfee, AJ Hawk
Frequency: Weekly
Average Show Length: 120 Minutes

Description:
Pat McAfee and AJ Hawk join Barstool Sports' Jerry Thornton to answer the question, "What would it sound like if two NFL greats and a football writer got together to discuss everything in the NFL worth talking about and lots more stuff that isn't?"

You May Also Like:
Heartland Radio: Presented by The Pat McAfee Show, Starting 9, Young & Happy, Fore Play, Barstool Rundown

The Ringer NFL Show
Hosts: Robert Mays, Kevin Clark, Mallory Rubin, Tate Frazier
Frequency: Weekly
Average Show Length: 50 Minutes

Description:
The Ringer NFL Show features a rotating group of Ringer NFL experts, including Michael Lombardi, Robert Mays, Kevin Clark, and Danny Kelly. The show will also feature ex-players and coaches, among others, as guests.

You May Also Like:
The Woj Pod, The Lowe Post, The Bill Barnwell Show, The Chronicles of Redick, Jalen & Jacoby

Jalen & Jacoby
Hosts: Jalen Rose, David Jacoby
Frequency: Daily
Average Show Length: 15 Minutes

Description:
Jalen Rose and David Jacoby give the people what they want, breaking down sports and pop culture as only they can.

The Tony Kornheiser Show
Host: Tony Kornheiser
Frequency: Daily
Average Show Length: 60 Minutes

Description:
Daily talk show that starts with sports and quickly moves into politics, current events, entertainment and, really, whatever happens to be on Tony's mind that day. The format of the show—regular sit-in guests with familiar interviews and segments—highlights not only the unique perspective of Tony Kornheiser but also the expertise of his network of friends.

You May Also Like:
PTI, The Ringer NFL Show, Against All Odds with Cousin Sal, Channel 33, The Watch

MeatEater Podcast
Host: Steven Rinella
Frequency: Weekly
Average Show Length: 120 Minutes

Description:
The MeatEater Podcast covers hunting, fishing, wildlife, and wild foods with humor, irreverence, and plenty of unexpected viewpoints and surprising trivia.

You May Also Like:
Nock On, Keep Hammering with Cameron Hanes, Hunt Talk Radio

Off The Bench with Kanell and Bell
Hosts: Danny Kanell, Raja Bell
Frequency: Daily
Average Show Length: 60 Minutes

Description:
Danny and Raja combined to come off the bench 241 times in their 18 years in the pros, now they're coming off the bench and behind the microphone 3 times a week.

TECHNOLOGY

2018 Technology Top Pick
TED Radio Hour
Host: Guy Raz
Frequency: Weekly
Average Show Length: 50 Minutes

The TED Radio Hour is a journey through fascinating ideas: astonishing inventions, fresh approaches to old problems, new ways to think and create. Based on Talks given by riveting speakers on the world-renowned TED stage, each show is centered on a common theme — such as the source of happiness, crowd-sourcing innovation, power shifts, or inexplicable connections

You May Also Like:
This American Life, Stuff You Should Know, Radiolab, Freakonomics Radio, TED Talks Daily

Reply All
Hosts: PJ Vogt, Alex Goldman
Frequency: Weekly
Average Show Length: 40 Minutes

Description:
A podcast about the internet' that is actually an unfailingly original exploration of modern life and how to survive it. The Guardian. Hosted by PJ Vogt and Alex Goldman, from Gimlet.

You May Also Like:
Radiolab Presents: More Perfect, 99% Invisible, Invisibilia, Embedded, Death, Sex & Money

WSJ The Future of Everything
Host: Various
Frequency: Weekly
Average Show Length: 20 Minutes

Description:
 A look ahead from The Wall Street Journal. How science and technology are revolutionizing business, industry, culture and society.

You May Also Like:
Undiscovered, Masters of Scale with Reid Hoffman, Part-Time Genius, Exchanges at Goldman Sachs, Masters in Business.

The freeCodeCamp Podcast
Host: Quincy Larson
Frequency: Daily
Average Show Length: 15 Minutes

Description:
The official podcast of the freeCodeCamp open source community. Learn to code with free online courses, programming projects, and interview preparation for developer jobs.

TEDTalks Technology
Host: Various
Frequency: Weekly
Average Show Length: 10 Minutes

Description:
Some of the world's leading inventors and researchers share demos, breakthroughs and visions onstage at the TED conference, TEDx events and partner events around the world.

You May Also Like:
TechStuff, Comedy Central Stand-Up, HBR IdeaCast, The HBR Channel, This Week in Tech

Why'd You Push That Button?
Hosts: Kaitlyn Tiffany, Ashley Carman
Frequency: Weekly
Average Show Length: 30 Minutes

Description:
Why'd You Push That Button examines the choices technology forces us to make, through interviews with consumers, developers, friends, and strangers.

You May Also Like:
Too Embarrassed to Ask, Tomorrow with Joshua Topolsky, Recode Media with Peter Kafka, Recode Replay, The Engadget Podcast

The Future According to Now
Host: Various
Frequency: Weekly
Average Show Length: 15 Minutes

Description:
The Future According to Now is a podcast from Fidelity Investments and Atlantic.

You May Also Like:
Outside the Box, Outside The Box Podcast, Got Science?

Note to Self
Host: Monoush Zomorodi
Frequency: Weekly
Average Show Length: 40 Minutes

Description:
Is your phone watching you? Can wexting make you smarter?
Are your kids real? These and other essential quandaries facing
anyone trying to preserve their humanity in the digital age. Join host
Manoush Zomorodi for your weekly reminder to question everything.

You May Also Like:
Reply All, Surprisingly Awesome, Undone, Science Vs, Heavyweight

Vector
Host: Rene Ritchie
Frequency: Daily
Average Show Length: 40 Minutes

Description:
Vector is a daily podcast by Apple analyst and tech critic Rene
Ritchie.

You May Also Like:
iMore, Android, CrackBerry.com, Windows

WSJ Tech News Briefing
Host: The Wall Street Journal
Frequency: Daily
Average Show Length: 5 Minutes

Description:
Stay informed on the latest trends with daily insights on what's hot
and happening in the world of technology. Listen to our reporters
discuss notable company news, new tech gadgets, personal
technology updates, app features, start-up highlights and more.

You May Also Like:
Bloomberg Surveillance, FT News, Marketplace Tech, Decrypted

Learn to Code With Me
Host: Laurence Bradford
Frequency: Weekly
Average Show Length: 30 Minutes

Description:
The Learn to Code With Me podcast, created by Laurence Bradford, is for aspiring techies and self-taught coders looking to transition into the tech industry. Want actionable insights on how you can get paid for your coding skills? Then you're in the right place!

You May Also Like:
CodeNewbie , Start Here: Web Development, Coding Blocks - Patterns, Architecture, Software Engineering Daily

BuzzFeed's Internet Explorer
Hosts: Ryan Broderick, Katie Notopoulos
Frequency: Weekly
Average Show Length: 60 Minutes

Description:
BuzzFeed editors Ryan Broderick and Katie Notopoulos explore the weirdest corners of the internet, so you don't have to.

You May Also Like:
TLDR, Sampler, Who? Weekly, The Nod, This Is Actually Happening

TechStuff
Host: Jonathan Strickland
Frequency: Weekly
Average Show Length: 60 Minutes

Description:
Join host Jonathan Strickland as he explores the people behind the tech, the companies that market it and how technology affects our lives and culture.

You May Also Like:
This Week in Tech, The Tech Guy, TEDTalks Technology

The Tech Guy
Host: Leo Laporte
Frequency: Weekly
Average Show Length: 120 Minutes

Description:
No one does a better job of explaining technology, computers, and the Internet than Leo Laporte. This feed contains the full audio of his twice weekly radio talk show as heard on stations all over the US on the Premiere Radio Networks.

You May Also Like:
iMore show, TechStuff, Daily Tech News Show, The Upgrade by Lifehacker, MacCast

This Week in Tech
Host: Leo Laporte
Frequency: Weekly
Average Show Length: 120 Minutes

Description:
Your first podcast of the week is the last word in tech. Join the top tech pundits in a roundtable discussion of the latest trends in high tech.

You May Also Like:
The Vergecast, No Agenda, TechStuff, Daily Tech News Show, iMore Show

a16z
Host: Andreessen Horowitz
Frequency: Weekly
Average Show Length: 30 Minutes

Description:
The a16z Podcast discusses tech and culture trends, news, and the future -- especially as 'software eats the world'. It features industry experts, business leaders, and other interesting thinkers and voices from around the world.

Moonshot
Host: Kristofor Lawson, Andrew Moon
Frequency: Weekly
Average Show Length: 30 Minutes

Description:
Unearth seemingly impossible ideas and the crazy people that believe they can make them happen. These are ideas like self-driving cars and going to Mars, that are about to change the future as we know it.

You May Also Like:
Space Nuts, Physical Attraction, BéaCast, Space Boffins Podcast, from the Naked Scientists, Space Boffins

Recode Decode, hosted by Kara Swisher
Host: Recode
Frequency: Weekly
Average Show Length: 15 Minutes

Description:
One of tech's most prominent journalists, Kara Swisher is known for her insightful reporting and straight-shooting style. Listen in as she hosts hard-hitting interviews about the week in tech with influential business leaders and outspoken personalities from media, politics and more.

You May Also Like:
a16z, Ctrl-Walt-Delete, Exponent, The Vergecast, Masters of Scale with Reid Hoffman

Tales from the Crypt
Host: Marty Bent
Frequency: Weekly
Average Show Length: 90 Minutes

Description:
Curious to learn more about Bitcoin and the other cryptoassets created in its wake? Navigate these new, scary waters.

Too Embarrassed to Ask
Hosts: Kara Swisher, Lauren Goode
Frequency: Weekly
Average Show Length: 45 Minutes

Description:
Technology doesn't need to be confusing, though too often it is.
Do you have tech questions that you're too embarrassed to ask?
Kara Swisher of Recode and Lauren Goode of The Verge have the
answers.

You May Also Like:
Ctrl-Walt-Delete, The Vergecast, What's Tech?, Why'd You Push That
Button?, Exponent

The Vergecast
Hosts: Nilay Patel, Dieter Bohn
Frequency: Weekly
Average Show Length: 90 Minutes

Description:
The Vergecast is your source for an irreverent and informative look
at what's happening right now (and next) in the world of technology
and gadgets. Hosted by Nilay Patel and Dieter Bohn, alongside a
cavalcade of tech luminaries, Vergecast is the only podcast you
need to make sense of the week in tech news. And your life.

You May Also Like:
Too Embarrassed to Ask, The Talk Show With John Gruber, Recode
Decode, hosted by Kara Swisher, Accidental Tech Podcast, iMore
show

Developing iOS 11 Apps with Swift
Host: Paul Hegarty
Frequency: Daily
Average Show Length: 60 Minutes

Description:
Tools and APIs required to build applications for the iPhone and

iPad platforms using the iOS SDK. User interface design for mobile devices and unique user interactions using multi-touch technologies. Object-oriented design using model-view-controller paradigm, memory management, Swift programming language.

You May Also Like:
iPad and iPhone Application, How to Think, Programming, Developing Apps for iOS, Entrepreneurial Thought

iMore show
Hosts: Serenity Caldwell, Rene Ritchie
Frequency: Weekly
Average Show Length: 60 Minutes

Description:
 iPhone, iPad, Mac — for everything Apple and beyond. Learn more. Be more. iMore!

You May Also Like:
MacBreak Weekly, Happy Hour, MacCast, iOS Today, AppleInsider Podcast

This Week in Machine Learning & AI Podcast
Host: Sam Charrington
Frequency: Weekly
Average Show Length: 60 Minutes

Description:
The week's most interesting and important stories from the worlds of machine learning and artificial intelligence. We discuss the latest developments in research, technology, and business, and explore interesting projects from across the web. Technologies covered include: machine learning, artificial intelligence, deep learning, natural language processing, neural networks, analytics, big data and more.

You May Also Like:
Learning Machines 101, Machine Learning Guide, Talking Machines, Linear Digressions, The AI Podcast

Software Engineering Daily
Host: Jeff Meyerson
Frequency: Daily
Average Show Length: 60 Minutes

Description:
Technical interviews about software topics.

You May Also Like:
Software Engineering Radio , The Changelog, Coding Blocks -
Patterns, Architecture, Programming Throwdown, All JavaScript
Podcasts

Security Now
Host: Steve Gibson
Frequency: Weekly
Average Show Length: 120 Minutes

Description:
Steve Gibson, the man who coined the term spyware and created
the first anti-spyware program, creator of Spinrite and ShieldsUP,
discusses the hot topics in security today with Leo Laporte.

You May Also Like:
Paul's Security Weekly, Defensive Security Podcast - Malware,
Hacking, Cyber Security & Infosec, SANS Internet Storm Center, The
CyberWire, Risky Business

State Of The Art
Host: Ethan Appleby
Frequency: Daily
Average Show Length: 30 Minutes

Description:
Join host Ethan Appleby each week as he interviews leaders who
are at the forefront of technology's role in the art world. Because
tech is not only changing the way artists create, it's bringing radical
change in the way all of us interact with art.

Exponent
Host: Ben Thompson, James Allworth
Frequency: Weekly
Average Show Length: 60 Minutes

Description:
In this program we seek to explore the massive effect technology is having not just on technology companies, but also on society as a whole. Ben Thompson is the author of Stratechery, a blog about the business and strategy of technology. James Allworth is the co-author with Clay Christensen of "How Will You Measure Your Life" and a writer for the Harvard Business Review.

You May Also Like:
a16z, Recode Decode, The Twenty Minute VC, Recode Media

Marketplace Tech with Molly Wood
Host: Ben Brock Johnson
Frequency: Daily
Average Show Length: 5 Minutes

Description:
Marketplace Tech host Molly Wood helps listeners understand the business behind the technology that's rewiring our lives. From how tech is changing the nature of work to the unknowns of venture capital to the economics of outer space, this weekday show breaks ideas, telling the stories of modern life through our digital economy. Marketplace Tech is part of the Marketplace portfolio of public radio programs broadcasting nationwide, which additionally includes Marketplace, Marketplace Morning Report and Marketplace Weekend.

You May Also Like:
WSJ Tech News Briefing, Daily Tech News Show, Tech News Weekly (MP3), PRI's The World: Latest Edition, MarketFoolery

WANT TO START YOUR OWN PODCAST?

Download Podcasting Pro Basics FREE at
PodcastingPro.com/freebook